BEVERLEY McLACHLIN

THE LEGACY OF A SUPREME COURT CHIEF JUSTICE

BEVERLEY McLACHLIN

THE LEGACY OF A SUPREME COURT CHIEF JUSTICE

IAN GREENE AND PETER McCORMICK

JAMES LORIMER & COMPANY LTD., PUBLISHERS
TORONTO

James Lorimer & Company Ltd., Publishers acknowledges funding support from the Ontario Arts Council (OAC), an agency of the Government of Ontario. We acknowledge the support of the Canada Council for the Arts, which last year invested $153 million to bring the arts to Canadians throughout the country. This project has been made possible in part by the Government of Canada and with the support of Ontario Creates.

Cover design: Tyler Cleroux
Cover image: Photograph © Jean-Marc Carisse

Library and Archives Canada Cataloguing in Publication

Title: Beverley McLachlin : the legacy of a Supreme Court chief justice / Ian Greene and Peter McCormick.
Other titles: Legacy of a Supreme Court chief justice
Names: Greene, Ian, author. | McCormick, Peter James, author.
Description: Includes bibliographical references and index.
Identifiers: Canadiana (print) 20190138939 | Canadiana (ebook) 20190139161 | ISBN 9781459414402 (hardcover) | ISBN 9781459414419 (epub)
Subjects: LCSH: McLachlin, Beverley, 1943- | LCSH: Judges—Canada—Biography. | LCSH: Canada. Supreme Court. | LCGFT: Biographies.
Classification: LCC KE8248.M36 G74 2019 | LCC KF345.Z95.M36 G74 2019 kfmod | DDC 347.71/03534092—dc23

James Lorimer & Company Ltd., Publishers
117 Peter Street, Suite 304
Toronto, ON, Canada
M5V 0M3
www.lorimer.ca

Printed and bound in Canada.

Contents

To the McLachlin Court

Introduction

I truly believe that the fact that I am in this position today is more than anything else a testament to the justice of Canadian society — a society where people without money, or connections, or the usual gender for a certain job, will be allowed to do it, and having done it, will be allowed to succeed. When I was growing up, there were few women lawyers, and no women judges. But there was an increasing awareness that fairness required equal opportunities for women, and that the law must work to ensure this. More than anything that I could personally bring to the task, I am the beneficiary of that sense of fairness, and of the laws and practices that cast it in concrete form. Today's youth, I hope, will benefit in even greater measure.[1]

These were Beverley McLachlin's words at an event organized by her friends and colleagues in Vancouver to celebrate her appointment as chief justice of Canada in 2000. McLachlin, the first woman chief justice of the Supreme Court of Canada, also became the longest-serving chief justice, retiring in 2017, and arguably one of the most effective judges the court has had in terms of the advancement of the rule of law[2] and human rights, clarity of writing, leadership and the promotion of collegiality.

Her career was not one that she planned for herself. If she had been able to set her own life course when she was in her thirties, she would have combined teaching law with writing novels, along with occasional work as a litigation lawyer.[3] She would have spent more time on family outings and her hobbies. But her personal qualities of collegiality, hard work, insight, impartiality, intelligence and down-to-earth humility quickly brought her to the attention of senior judges and politicians.

Judicial decisions she has written or co-authored have helped to define us as Canadians. This book highlights those decisions that have had the greatest impact on Canadian society. Her job was to consider all the arguments as impartially as possible and then make a decision that could best be supported by the law and the evidence, taking into account the constitutional tradition of the rule of law, along with reasonability, compassion and humanity — what she referred to as "conscious objectivity."[4]

She loved her four decades as a judge.[5] Every new case had human stories attached, and from the time she could read, she was fascinated by all kinds of tales of human adventure.[6] As a judge writing decisions, she could only relate those parts of the stories that were relevant to legal issues; after retiring, she finally had licence to fully disclose her story-telling passion.[7] During her last year as a judge, one that saw her author more than her average yearly number of decisions, she wrote her first novel: "I started tentatively, getting up at 5:30 a.m. before regular work to see what would happen. Soon the story took over — the characters, the plot, the pathos and the joy — elements I had absorbed over the decades now fused into something new, something true but not-true. To my astonishment, the result found a publisher."[8] The novel was published on May 1, 2018, towards the end of the six months judges receive after retirement to complete writing their decisions.[9]

This book links Beverley McLachlin, the person, with Beverley McLachlin, the judge. It is not a traditional biography in that it does not seek to chronicle every aspect of her life and career. We are social scientists interested in shedding light on Canada's rich judicial and legal culture. Our purpose is to place McLachlin in that context.

We have both studied the leading decisions of the Supreme Court of Canada and the judicial decision-making process during our academic careers.[10] As well, we both grew up in rural Alberta and so are familiar with the lifestyle there during the 1950s and 1960s. We both attended the University of Alberta, which Beverley McLachlin attended four or five years ahead of us. Writing about her intrigued us because of these links.

McLachlin's story is a fascinating one. It begins in the 1940s and 1950s on a ranch nestled in the foothills of the Rocky Mountains west of Pincher Creek, Alberta, where young Beverley Gietz made the most of every moment and found her way to the University of Alberta in Edmonton. As a university student, she explored varied interests in law, philosophy, journalism and the arts. As a married woman practising law in Edmonton, Fort St. John and Vancouver and then as a mother teaching at the University of British Columbia law school, she honed her time management skills to achieve work/life balance. She had just begun to explore the corridors of academia when she was plucked out of it by the movement to appoint more women judges.

Widowed at a young age, she rose rapidly through the judicial ranks and was an associate justice of the Supreme Court of Canada by the time she was forty-six. On the Supreme Court she was involved in some of the central issues of the 1990s: interpretation of the *Charter of Rights and Freedoms*, Aboriginal rights, Quebec secession and others. She characteristically wanted to hear all the arguments surrounding these complex questions and choose the most compelling solution.

Elevated to chief justice in 2000, she turned a divisive court into one of the most collegial and reflective institutions of its type in the world. In her long tenure in the "centre chair," she contributed significantly to decisions dealing with assisted dying, prostitution, safe injection sites, prisoners' voting rights, Canada's obligations to child soldiers and Aboriginal rights, among other issues. Faced with an attack on her independence and integrity by Prime Minister Stephen Harper, she never lost her cool in defending herself, the Canadian judicial system and the rule of law.

Through it all she has remained a human being who valued having lifelong friends, and who could think, write and make a contribution to society.

We are grateful to Beverley McLachlin for an interview that she gave us on April 9, 2018, to which we refer in the pages that follow.

1

Early Years

Chief Justice McLachlin was reminded of her prairie upbringing several times a day. In her Supreme Court office hung a painting depicting the prairie and mountain landscape near Pincher Creek, though it ended up there more by accident than by design.[1] We see reflections of McLachlin's roots five decades later in the impact that she had on the Supreme Court and her commitment to the rule of law and empathetic, evidence-based decision-making as a Supreme Court justice.

Born in 1943, Beverley Marian Gietz (pronounced geetz) was the oldest of five children born to Eleanora Kruschell (1920–1972) and Ernest Gietz (1915–1977). Beverley's younger siblings were Leonard (1945), Conrad (1947), Judi (1954) and Ronald (1960).

Ernest Gietz was born in the tiny village of Lipno, now in Poland but at the time part of Germany.[2] He was one of fourteen children in an ethnically German family.[3] The family had been moderately prosperous in Europe, but because of the unstable political and economic situation — at one time they hid a Jewish family in their basement to protect them from a pogrom — they immigrated to Canada in 1927.[4]

Pincher Creek was an "improbable" place to settle for Beverley's father's family, and she has "no idea" why they ended up there.[5] But like so many prairie settlers in the early twentieth century, they decided to put their old-world experience to use and farm in the new world. They bought a farm with a house on it three or four kilometres east of the town centre. Beverley lived there with her parents and younger siblings until she was eleven, except for one year that the family spent in Alberta's Peace River district, 700 kilometres to the north.

Beverley McLachlin's life before she was twelve was fairly typical for a girl growing up on a farm near a prairie town in the 1940s, except for the family's one-year sojourn in the north. That move and return would have meant leaving behind friends and familiar surroundings twice, having to adapt to change. Later, as her career took her through three court levels in British Columbia and from associate justice to chief justice on the Supreme Court of Canada, her ability to adapt to change stood out as one of her strengths.

Pincher Creek was established in 1878 as a North-West Mounted Police post, and settlers began to farm in the area a few years later. It was incorporated as a town in 1906, and in the 1940s had a population of a little over a thousand. The town and the farms within a reasonable distance were connected to the electrical grid. In town, milk was delivered by horse and cart, and on the farms, most families ate produce from their own land.

Because their farm was close to town, the Gietz family was not isolated. There were frequent visits to town for supplies and social events. School was within walking distance whenever the school bus was not available. Pincher Creek also had a movie theatre. Beverley and her friends would have seen all the Disney movies popular at the time, as well as classics such as *Heidi*, featuring nine-year-old child star Shirley Temple.[6] *Heidi* was a favourite among Beverley and her friends,[7] both because of the scenes in the Swiss

Alps that might have been shot near Pincher Creek and because it whetted their imagination about what the world beyond their own idyllic landscape might be like.

On the farm, there was always plenty for the kids to do, from daily chores assigned by their parents to playing with the animals and exploring the land. In addition, as the oldest child, Beverley helped take care of her brothers and sisters. On Sundays, the children attended church school while their parents participated in the church service. Beverley's grandparents were Evangelical Lutherans, and she was brought up in that tradition.[8]

The late 1940s saw the start of the baby boom, and school populations soon exploded.[9] The basics of reading, writing and arithmetic were stressed, and the strap was still used for corporal punishment. The old school buildings were permeated with the odour of oiled floors and wax crayons. Children learned to print in the early grades, and were taught cursive writing beginning in grade three or four. Penmanship was important, and school desks had inkwells or ink jars into which students dipped their pen nibs. Fountain pens were not allowed until a certain level of proficiency had been achieved.[10] The school curriculum was updated over time to include more Canadian content.[11]

Like many small communities in Alberta, the Pincher Creek area was settled over several decades by immigrant families from various parts of the U.K. and continental Europe, and during Beverley McLachlin's formative years the area still had a pioneer spirit. The last years of the Second World War and the decade that followed were a time when most families in rural Alberta struggled to make ends meet, but they did so by supporting one another, no matter the ethnicity or religion of their neighbours.

In addition to hosting immigrants from diverse parts of Europe, there were several Hutterite colonies near Pincher Creek.[12] The Hutterites, part of the Anabaptist tradition, are communal farmers with up to 150 people in each colony. They are early adopters of modern farming techniques, and each colony has modern machinery repair facilities that they welcome their neighbours to use. The Piikani Nation reserve is located about twenty kilometres east of Pincher Creek, and the Kainai reserve, the largest in terms of area in Canada, is located about forty-five kilometres farther east.[13]

Ernest Gietz employed men from the Piikani reserve from time to time. McLachlin recalled a day when a large Indigenous family was visiting and was invited into the house for cake to celebrate Ernest's birthday. Years later, when McLachlin was in Pincher Creek for a high school reunion, an Indigenous man presented her with a set of pearl earrings that he had set himself. He had been one of the children invited in for cake. He told her, "Your parents were the most wonderful people, and I will never forget them . . . It was the first time I ever went into a white person's home."[14]

According to McLachlin, "It would be hard to grow up in such a setting and think there's only one right way to live or one religion or one way of doing things that's exclusively correct or even greatly superior to other ways . . . When you grow up in a small but very diverse community, it inculcates a certain breadth of acceptance."[15] It is no wonder that McLachlin was able to write so clearly about the legitimate grievances of First Nations people later on as chief justice,[16] and to take into consideration the differences among various Hutterite communities in her decision on the Hutterian Brethren.[17]

In his early twenties, Ernest Gietz attended a Bible college, and he worked for a short time in a ministry in Barrhead in northern Alberta. He was a lifelong volunteer in churches, sometimes as a lay minister, but also harboured a lifelong distrust of organized religion. As an adult, he felt uncomfortable being associated with just one Christian tradition. According to McLachlin, "He was quite religious, but not in an organized religious way. He was a free thinker, I guess, so he never got involved with a denomination. He liked thinking about religion. He was a very intellectual person, a very smart person. He sometimes got called in to give a sermon."[18]

Ernest met Eleanora Kruschell while on his northern ministry near Barrhead, and they married in 1942. Eleanora had been born in Compeer, Alberta (northeast of Calgary near the Saskatchewan border). She had wanted to go to university and become a writer, but her hopes were dashed when she had to stay home to take care of her mother, who had become ill. In his extensive profile of McLachlin in *The Globe and Mail* on her retirement, Sean Fine noted that Beverley's "drive to get an education was driven in part by her mother's failed dream of studying at university. 'I identified very early with her aspirations, and her disappointment.'"[19]

After Beverley finished grade six, her family sold the farm east of Pincher Creek and bought land far west of the area. Beverley's life changed dramatically. The ranch was south and west of Pincher Creek near the headwaters of Mill Creek, about thirty kilometres north of Waterton Lakes National Park.[20] The property was about as far southwest of Pincher Creek as anyone in Alberta could settle without encroaching on the forest reserve or the national park. Ernest established a sawmill, farm and ranch. The wilderness location proved to be both an adventure and a challenge for Beverley.

To begin with, the family lived in an old log house with no electricity and no running water. Perishable food was kept in an ice box; there was an outhouse in the backyard: "And if someone got a little too extravagant with the toilet paper, the pages of the old Eaton catalogue came in handy."[21] Light was provided by kerosene lanterns and candles, which children weren't often allowed to handle. Water was hauled into the house from the well, and in the winter the buckets of water would freeze overnight.[22] Heat was provided by a wood-burning stove, and the wood had to be chopped and the ashes taken out.

Referring to the house, McLachlin recalled that "it wasn't very big, but I kind of liked it."[23] The house consisted of three rooms — one big room, perhaps five metres square, a bedroom for the parents and another one for the children. "The big room had the kitchen along one side — a wood stove, a big oak table, and a sitting area . . . I think it was pretty typical of Canadian log houses in that era."[24] The family bath was prepared in a wash tub with water that had been heating on the stove all day. The youngest child had the first bath. In Sean Fine's description, "A little hot water was added for the next, and the next, all the way up to the oldest, Beverley, and then her mother and father."[25]

Because the ranch was so remote, there was no school bus service, and Beverley completed grade seven by correspondence. She thought the quality of the correspondence courses she took was excellent and attributes some of her writing skills to this correspondence experience.[26] A cousin of Eleanora Gietz was a senior administrator in Alberta's correspondence school branch, and so Eleanora and Ernest were confident that correspondence school would serve the children well as a temporary measure. "You were given one main teacher who assigned books and exercises and for whom you wrote little essays and so on . . . And it was a very serious education . . . They made you write out everything."[27] Beverley enjoyed her correspondence courses and worked on them diligently, so much so that she completed everything by Christmas: "I had nothing else to do, and it was very lonely out there."[28] Beverley missed the companionship of friends, and persuaded her parents to find a family that she could board with in town so that she could attend grade eight in Pincher Creek.

When Beverley was thirteen, the property was connected to the electrical grid, and she helped her mother and father design a new house that was constructed from timbers her father milled. One of Beverley's close friends in high school was Diana Reed, and occasionally Diana would have overnight visits with the Gietz family: "Beverley's room seemed like a scene from the movie *Heidi* . . . I remember being with her and looking out the window at the mountains and the stars."[29]

At the ranch, Beverley learned to entertain herself by riding a horse, hiking through the woods and mountains and observing wildlife. She learned independence and self-reliance.[30] The family

obtained a piano for the house, and Beverley learned to play it, taking occasional piano lessons in Pincher Creek. She loved reading.
Because her parents appreciated literature, the house had a small
collection of diverse books, and she read them all:

> *I have always loved stories. The love began with child-*
> *hood, as such loves usually do. Fairy tales of princesses in*
> *castles and trolls on bridges, enthralling and frightening*
> *and drive-you-under-the-covers scary. Old Testament*
> *sagas full of romance, war and warnings of dire things to*
> *come. So enthralled was I with stories that on occasion I*
> *would turn my childish hand to chronicles of heroes dis-*
> *appearing down rabbit holes, Alice-like, to discover new*
> *worlds of magic and adventure. My mother tossed them*
> *out with the weekly trash, which is doubtless where they*
> *belonged, but to this day I remember with pleasure the*
> *exhilarated hours I spent scribbling them at the dining-*
> *room table.*[31]

Biblical stories were one of the topics of discussion at the ranch.
According to McLachlin, "There was a strong tradition of debate
and study. You were always reading the Scriptures and talking
about them . . . And so I grew up with lots of philosophizing and
debate. I think that had an impact on my mind as I grew up."[32]
Years later, while studying philosophy at the University of Alberta,
McLachlin discovered Joseph Campbell,[33] whose analysis of stories
from various religions shows how these narratives form meaning
for those willing to go beyond literal interpretation. It may be that
Ernest's free thinking helped to sow the seeds for McLachlin's later
admiration for Campbell.[34]

Beginning in grade eight, Beverley discovered the local library
in Pincher Creek, and between grades eight and twelve she "con-
sumed"[35] its contents. She started off with "Nancy Drew — smart
girls chasing down gentle thieves — and the Hardy Boys — teenage

sleuths who once rode the El in Chicago to intercept marauders and keep the city safe."[36] Once she had read everything in the juvenile section, she started reading from the adult section, such as books by the Victorian novelist Anthony Trollope. The matrons of the library "tactfully kept it to themselves."[37]

Beverley's voracious reading was, in part, inspired by her mother's example. McLachlin recalled that her mother "was always telling stories, reading stories, talking about the books she'd read as a girl — all the Lucy Maud Montgomery books. She lived a rich life of the imagination through fiction."[38]

In grade nine, which was the start of high school in Pincher Creek, Beverley lived with about thirty other country kids in a dormitory provided by the school board.[39] "The girls lived on the second floor, the boys lived on the third floor," recalled Diana Reed. "The main floor was for eating, cooking, and living quarters for the guardians."[40] One of the punishments for misbehaviour was to peel a five-gallon pail of potatoes every day for a week.[41] The high school was named after Matthew Halton, the Canadian Broadcasting Corporation's World War II correspondent who was born in Pincher Creek in 1904. Students from the Piikani reserve began to attend Matthew Halton High during Beverley's grade twelve year. One of those students was Peter Yellow Horn, who later became chief of the Piikani First Nation and a key figure leading the protest over construction of the Oldman River Dam on the Piikani reserve.[42] "I had more knowledge of our Indigenous brothers and sisters than a lot of people might have," McLachlin observed.[43]

Beverley began high school at a time when the Alberta government had started shutting down small country schools and centralizing education facilities in relatively larger communities like Pincher Creek. Matthew Halton High School was built to accommodate both town and country students. Throughout her high school years, there were two classes in each grade — one class for the "town" kids and the other for the "country" kids, like Beverley and Diana, who were joining the enlarged school for the first time. Town kids could get involved in school sports teams that played against other schools on weekends while the country kids were more limited, as they went home on weekends to stay with their families. Nevertheless, Beverley participated in high school sports as much as her schedule permitted.

During her high school years, Beverley contributed to the year-book and to other student publications. She sang in the school choir and performed in school musicals. The most intricate work the choir performed was Handel's *Messiah*,[44] and the most challenging musical production was Gilbert and Sullivan's *The Gondoliers*. Beverley wrote for the school newspaper, the *Halton Highlights*. She developed a reputation as an excellent writer, although one teacher was concerned that Beverley had a selective memory.[45] Going home on weekends meant she was in charge of her growing younger siblings — another opportunity to hone her leadership qualities.

According to high school classmates, Beverley was a very positive young woman who got along well with other students and worked hard to do her best in all her classes. "Her favourite word was 'terrific," according to Diana Reed.[46] Beverley and her close friends were determined to go to university but knew they could not achieve that goal without the assistance of scholarships, as their families did not have the necessary financial resources.

Beverley's parents encouraged her to do well at school and to get as much advanced education as she could. She graduated from high school in 1961 with the highest grades in the school. In addition to being presented with a wristwatch for that achievement, she won a bursary from the Alberta Hotelmen's Association worth $500 — a large amount in those days — which enabled her to enroll at the University of Alberta in Edmonton to "study education and foreign languages."[47]

During her summer prior to university, Beverley won a Canada Council Award that enabled her, along with nine other top Alberta high school graduates, to tour parts of Canada east of Alberta. At an awards ceremony in Pincher Creek in September 1961, Beverley "related many experiences, stating she was most impressed with Stratford. Among other things, the group toured the theatre, visited museums and the National Drama School, where they met actors and actresses and witnessed three plays."[48]

Beverley's Canada Council Award trip was an eye-opening experience. Growing up in an inspiringly beautiful location north of Waterton National Park is enviable. Being introduced to parts of the rest of Canada at an impressionable age would surely have whetted her already keen appetite for learning more about the rest of the world.

Beverley's high school friends have enjoyed socializing with her over the years at high school reunions and have observed that she is the "same Beverley that she has always been — down to earth, positive, outgoing and friendly."[49] At one reunion, she managed to rise early and leave her hotel — before her security guards were awake — to watch a cattle branding with her friends.[50]

Beverley McLachlin's growing-up years around Pincher Creek taught her self-reliance, perseverance in resolving problems, tolerance, compassion, writing skills and the beginnings of her philosophical reasoning skills. As Sean Fine reported, "Those early years bred in her that quality that defined her as a judge: a 'fierce independence,' in the words of Warren Winkler, who grew up in the area at the same time, and went on to become Chief Justice of Ontario."[51] She learned from her parents that "no matter how much education a person achieves, no matter what opportunities a person gets, what is important is who you are inside," said Reed. "Beverley McLachlin has a heart and soul filled with integrity."[52]

An example of Beverley's creativity in high school is this poem that she contributed to the *Halton Highlights*:

THE CALL OF THE WEST WIND

I can hear the west wind sighing
O'er the broad plains swiftly flying
Proud, and free.

O'er the sleeping plains she passes
Stirs to life the slumbering grasses
Beckons me.

From the Rockies she comes sweeping
Down a bismal chasm leaping
Swift and proud.

Splashing crystal down the mountain
Churning waters, foaming fountains,
Roaring loud.

O'er the forest now she's raging
Fast and furious throughout waging,
Cruel, unkind.

Groaning pines bemoan her fury
As she ever onward hurries
Unconfined.

O'er the clean-swept hills she's lashing
To the prairies swiftly flashing
Dust entombed.

Through the wheat fields, gently swaying
Bitter noon-day heat allaying
Whittling low.

I can hear the west wind sighing
O'er the broad plains swiftly flying
Proud, and free.

O'er the sleeping plains she passes
Stirs to life the slumbering grasses
Beckons me.

Carrying with her memories of the west wind, the plains of southern Alberta and the Rockies on the horizon, eighteen-year-old Beverley headed off to the University of Alberta in Edmonton, 500 kilometres to the north, in 1961. It was the start of a new adventure. She carried with her the educational achievements from Pincher Creek and the personal qualities developed during her upbringing in and around Pincher Creek: an insatiable curiosity about the nature of things and the desire for an accurate understanding; an empathy for people of all backgrounds and an aversion to their mistreatment; perseverance when confronted with challenges; and a spirit of self-reliance and determination to explore the potential of her abilities.

2

Edmonton to Vancouver

The contrast between life on a ranch at the foot of the Rocky Mountains and life in Edmonton — a rapidly growing city located far from the mountains — was dramatic for Beverley Gietz. Not only was the geography of Edmonton different from Pincher Creek, but so was the climate. Edmonton was much colder in the winter than southern Alberta, where winter temperatures were modified by warm Chinook winds.[1] On one hand, the change was alarming. On the other, it was an adventure like exploring the forests and mountains around her childhood home — something to be seized with prudent enthusiasm.

Edmonton had a population of 276,000 in 1961; ten years later, when McLachlin left for British Columbia, the city had grown to 436,000.[2] The oil boom was in full swing. Money was flowing into the provincial government's coffers from oil royalties. Some of these funds were used to build the Jubilee[3] Auditoriums in Edmonton and Calgary in 1955. These state-of-the-art concert halls, still in use today, made it possible for Edmonton and Calgary to attract talented musicians and conductors for their symphony orchestras. The Edmonton Opera Company was formed in 1963, and the Citadel Theatre was founded in Edmonton in 1965.

Alberta's political landscape was also beginning to change at that time. "Wild Bill" Hawrelak, who had been mayor of Edmonton in the 1950s but was forced to resign because of misconduct, was re-elected in 1963. Students protested his election, and riots ensued. A judge disqualified Hawrelak from office in 1965, a finding later upheld by the Supreme Court of Canada. During the 1960s, University of Alberta students organized numerous demonstrations against the war in Vietnam.

At the provincial level, Peter Lougheed became leader of the previously moribund Progressive Conservative Party in 1965, and his party won six seats in the legislature in 1967 with a good deal of student help. Lougheed's party absorbed most of the provincial Liberal Party, and even drew support from some erstwhile NDP backers, bringing to the surface a widespread hunger for change. In 1971 Lougheed's Conservatives defeated the Social Credit government that had been in office since 1935.

The 1960s were also a time of dramatic change in Canada and around the world. Federally, there were minority governments led by Conservative John Diefenbaker and Liberal Lester Pearson. There were intense debates over the new maple leaf flag, universal health care and the Canada Pension Plan. Canadians converged on Montreal for Expo 67. Pierre Trudeau became prime minister in 1968. The Quiet Revolution was taking hold in Quebec. René Lévesque spoke to university students in Edmonton after he left the Quebec Liberal Party to form the Mouvement Souveraineté-Association in 1967. A young Montreal poet named Leonard Cohen sang some of his poetry to an English class at the University of Alberta. Ian Tyson and Sylvia Fricker moved to southern Alberta, not far from Pincher Creek, and released the album *Four Strong Winds* in 1964. The civil rights movement in the United States was in full swing. Dr. Martin Luther King Jr. winner of the

Nobel Peace Prize in 1964, presented the CBC Massey Lecture in 1967. The next year he was assassinated. Neil Armstrong and Buzz Aldrin landed on the moon in 1969. Pierre Trudeau invoked the *War Measures Act* during the October Crisis of 1970. Jim Matkin, a classmate of Beverley McLachlin in law school, has highlighted the importance of the dramatic changes occurring in the 1960s for understanding the determination of university students at that time to make the world a better place through their careers.[4]

The University of Alberta, established in 1908, had approximately 12,000 students in 1961. Enrolment grew steadily during the 1960s and approached 20,000 by the end of the decade.[5] About half the students were from Edmonton and another two-fifths were from other parts of Alberta.[6] In the professional faculties, such as law and medicine, women represented a small minority, although the proportion of women in nearly all faculties grew substantially during the 1960s.[7]

THE UNIVERSITY OF ALBERTA

Beverley Gietz enrolled at the University of Alberta to study education and foreign languages,[8] but like many first-year students she soon changed her mind. She decided to pursue a degree in philosophy. She recalls that when she came to the University of Alberta, her "mind was a bit of a mess. It was very muddy."[9] Her degree in philosophy helped her to sort out her own ideas in a clear and logical way: "It helped me learn to order my ideas better . . . You have to be able to defend or analytically attack a position, and you have to be able to set out either process in clear terms that other people can understand."[10] The writings of the classic philosophers, from Plato to Locke, Rousseau and Montesquieu, provided students with some of the most engaging readings that they would encounter as undergraduates, and Beverley Gietz eagerly sought out readings that captured her imagination and curiosity. She commented that as a judge it was

*really valuable to have had acquaintance with some of
the great thinkers of our particular western civilization,
and other civilizations to the extent that you master
them. You realize the wisdom and the values that
have been preserved over thousands of years, and that
background informs how you understand the problems
before you.*[11]

She had "great professors"[12] in the philosophy department,
but undoubtedly one of her favourites was Anthony Mardiros.
According to a history of the department, Mardiros, "an Austra-
lian who had studied with Wittgenstein at Cambridge during the
Second World War, joined the Department in 1947 and became
Head in 1957."[13] Mardiros later wrote a book about William Irvine,
one of the pioneers of Canada's socialist movement and a founding
leader of the Co-operative Commonwealth Federation, forerunner
of the New Democratic Party.[14] Mardiros supervised McLachlin's
master's thesis in philosophy, a degree she completed at the same
time as her law degree.

Top undergraduate students tend to be engaged in outside
interests, and Beverley Gietz devoted her energies to at least two.
Her experience with the *Halton Highlights* in high school led her
to volunteer to write for the University of Alberta's *The Gateway*,
which prided itself on being one of the top university student
newspapers in Canada. True to her interest in the arts, she wrote
for the arts section. Ten years earlier, Peter Lougheed had written
for *The Gateway*'s sports section, and just prior to Beverley's time
with the publication, Joe Clark, a future prime minister, had been
the editor-in-chief. Clark was also the product of a small town in
southern Alberta — High River. In spite of rubbing shoulders with
the student newspaper's highly politicized staff and learning about
the socialist movement from Professor Mardiros, Beverley never
demonstrated much interest in becoming actively involved with
any political movement.

She was much more attracted to the arts and music. She joined the University of Alberta Mixed Chorus, a choir of some 100 students that toured parts of the province each spring. Auditions were required to be accepted into this renowned choir, and Beverley Gietz's experience singing *Messiah* and *The Gondoliers* in Pincher Creek, in addition to her having learned to read music through her piano lessons, proved helpful. The conductor of the Mixed Chorus was Richard Eaton, a legend in his time, under whose tutorship numerous musical careers were established. The Mixed Chorus had a lively social schedule for its members, including a pig roast on a farm near Edmonton in the fall, caroling at Edmonton hospitals before Christmas and a skating party on Whitemud Creek in the winter. McLachlin remembers the Mixed Chorus as a "wonderful institution,"[15] a highlight of her years at the University of Alberta.

During her undergraduate years, Beverley Gietz met Roderick (Rory) McLachlin, who was studying for his MA in biology at the University of Alberta. Recognizing Beverley's bright and logical mind, Rory suggested that she think about becoming a lawyer. As Kirk Makin has written, Rory persuaded her "that a tough-minded woman could break through the institutional barriers of the predominantly male legal profession."[16] Rory's mother, a medical doctor, provided an example.[17]

In 1965, Beverley wrote to Dean Wilbur Bowker of the law school to ask for an appointment to discuss whether she should apply to law school. When she arrived at his office for the appointment, he said, "Congratulations — you're accepted." Dean Bowker, one of the leading figures of the legal profession in Alberta, must have looked up her stellar undergraduate grades before the appointment. Beverley did not immediately confirm the acceptance.[18] In her usual cautious manner, she took some time to consider, and in the end attended law school.

Beverley Gietz and Rory McLachlin were married in 1967, during the summer after Beverley's second year of law school. By all reports, they had a happy marriage. They would make visits to the ranch at Pincher Creek to visit family, and Rory got on well with Beverley's friends.[19]

Beverley McLachlin had some excellent professors at law school. She studied torts from Dean Bowker, "who often scheduled extra classes on Saturday so we could study more cases, and we didn't complain."[20] She had Dr. Alex Smith for contracts and constitutional law, "who taught with such fervor that we thought, before the *Charter*, that the intricacies of [the Canadian division of powers] were fascinating."[21] Trevor Anderson, who wore his Oxford robes in class, taught property law; he later became dean of the law school at the University of Manitoba. Ivan Head, who taught international law, later became the legal and international affairs advisor to Prime Minister Pierre Trudeau.[22]

According to Matkin, Beverley's classmate, "Bev was a class leader from the beginning."[23] As a student anxious to learn, she tended to sit in the front row centre of each class, and she was always well prepared. Her examination answers were so well written that she was sometimes "asked to read to the rest of the class some of her answers for the benefit of the rest of us."[24] She formed study groups with other class members, and her cohort "had a reputation for studying more than partying."[25] During her law school years, her younger brother Leonard studied medicine at the University of Alberta.[26]

Beverley worked one summer in the office of Garth Turcott, who was the only lawyer in Pincher Creek and in 1966 became the first member of the NDP to be elected to the Alberta legislature. Turcott remembers her as being bright, hard-working and efficient, but notes she wasn't enthusiastic about pursuing either a career in law in Pincher Creek or a career in politics.[27]

During the summer after she completed her philosophy degree, and before attending law school, she got a job as a teaching assistant in the philosophy department being set up at the new University of Calgary, which became independent from the University of

Alberta in 1966. While working as a TA, she completed two gradu-
ate courses in philosophy. As an undergraduate, she had taken two
extra fourth-year philosophy courses which were combined gradu-
ate/undergraduate courses. During her last summer in law school,
she realized that she had actually completed all the coursework for
a master's degree, and to earn the degree she just needed to write a
thesis. She applied for and was offered a research grant "that paid
more than the [summer] job I had, so I took the grant and spent all
my time day and night writing the thesis."[28]

The subject that McLachlin chose for her thesis was the debate
about the nature of law between two legal philosophers who wrote
in the 1950s, H.L.A. Hart[29] and Lon Fuller.[30] Hart was a critic of the
rigid philosophy of "legal positivism" promoted by John Austin.[31]
The Austinian positivist approach, simply put, posits that the law is
that which is enacted by legislatures and good judges can apply the
law correctly and objectively. Hart criticized this approach as fail-
ing to recognize that laws can never cover every aspect of human
behaviour, and therefore even good judges have discretion in cases
that are not clear cut. McLachlin argued that Hart's approach was
really a revised, softer form of positivism that left little room for
morality to play a role.

Fuller, on the other hand, argued for a stronger role for morality in interpreting the law, the so-called "natural law" approach to
jurisprudence. In her conclusion, McLachlin agrees "with Hart in
his position that the relationship between law and morality is not
one of logical necessity. At the same time, however . . . [there are]
equally important ways in which law and morality intersect . . . The
resultant picture is that of a system of legal rules, distinct from, yet
in various ways supported by, moral rules and ideals."[32] As well,
she concluded that the most important way morality affects the law
is through judicial interpretation of the law.[33]

McLachlin's writing style in her thesis was little different from
her writing style years later as chief justice. Her thesis was clear,
concise and thorough. She described Hart's and Fuller's arguments

and their context objectively, analyzed their strengths and weaknesses, and then presented her own conclusions.

In 1968, Beverley McLachlin graduated with both her master's degree and her law degree. She won the gold medal for the highest grades in her graduating class in law.

LAWYERING IN EDMONTON

After graduating, McLachlin articled with the firm Wood, Moir, Hyde and Ross.[34] It was among the larger firms in Edmonton, though not the biggest. According to McLachlin, "It was a fine set of articles . . . We had thirteen or fourteen lawyers and some juniors. It did mainly litigation." She was admitted to the Alberta bar in 1969. The firm was impressed with her work, and after her articles asked her to stay on. She worked in that firm for another two and a half years.

FORT ST. JOHN

While Rory was working on his master's degree, he and members of his family entered into leases with the British Columbia government to develop agricultural land near Hudson's Hope, about ninety kilometres west of Fort St. John. After Rory completed his degree, he became the manager of the business, which meant he had to spend much more time in B.C., and the commute to Edmonton became more difficult. In 1971, Beverley decided to relocate to Fort St. John so that she and Rory could be together. Fort St. John was a small but rapidly growing community of about 8,000 in the Peace River area of northeastern British Columbia. After construction of the Alaska Highway during World War II, farmers began to settle in the area. Natural gas was discovered in the 1950s, which led to more expansion.

Given the shortage of lawyers in this frontier community, Beverley thought there was a good chance of a woman getting hired by a law firm. The problem was that the Law Society of British Columbia had a regulation that barred Alberta lawyers from practising in B.C. without having had three years of experience in Alberta after articling. McLachlin was six months shy of that requirement. She went to the Law Society of B.C. headquarters in Vancouver to plead for a dispensation. The person at the Law Society thought that an Alberta lawyer willing to practise in a remote location like Fort St. John deserved dispensation. He telephoned a lawyer acquaintance of his in Fort St. John, Dave Levis, and explained that the Law Society was "giving her a dispensation because anyone silly enough to go to Fort St. John deserved every break they could get."[35] Levis, anxious for another lawyer, hired her to work in his firm, Levis and Herdy.

Beverley and Rory purchased land outside Fort St. John, and Rory spent much of his time clearing the land.[36] Beverley became the first woman lawyer in Fort St. John. It was not common at that time for women either to become lawyers or to practise law. According to McLachlin, "Some people viewed women as an oddity . . . There were a lot of sexist comments. I just learned to ignore them. That was the other person's problem. I refused to make myself a victim."[37]

Although the McLachlins enjoyed the wilderness environment of Fort St. John, they found community life uninspiring. Nathan Nemetz,[38] then a justice on the B.C. Supreme Court, referred to Fort St. John as a "cultural wasteland" after one of his visits there.[39] The McLachlins missed the rich cultural life that they had left behind in Edmonton.

In 1972, the McLachlins decided to move to Vancouver, where Rory had been accepted into the Ph.D. program in forestry at the University of British Columbia. Beverley inquired at a couple of Vancouver firms, but they weren't hiring or weren't interested in her particular legal background. The McLachlins returned briefly to Fort St. John to ask for advice from her law firm colleagues. By this time, Dennis Mitchell had joined Levis and Herdy. Mitchell had articled with Bull, Housser and Tupper in Vancouver, and knew Wilfred (Bae) Wallace, a senior partner in that firm. Mitchell phoned Wallace, praised McLachlin's work in Fort St. John and explained the situation.[40] According to Wallace, Mitchell said, "I have a very able associate here who's going to Vancouver; her husband's going to be taking his Ph.D., and could you find work for her?"[41] Bull, Housser and Tupper was involved in preparing a major case involving B.C. Hydro for trial, and Wallace needed more help. He agreed to hire McLachlin and asked her to come to the office as soon as possible.

The year 1972 was a stressful one for McLachlin. Not only did she have to contend with the move to Vancouver and a new job, but her mother became terminally ill:

> I was in shock when my mother, at the age of fifty-one, was diagnosed with cancer. She had been suffering poor health for some time, but you never think it's going to be terminal, and it was shocking and difficult to come to grips with. She was in hospital in Calgary, and I used to fly out to see her from Vancouver every weekend or every other weekend. My younger sister was only eighteen at the time, and my little brother was only twelve. It was hard on everyone.[42]

Throughout this stressful period family members supported one another, and family ties grew closer. Eleanora Gietz died in December.

PRACTISING LAW IN VANCOUVER

When Beverley McLachlin reported for work at Bull, Housser and Tupper, she was told to join the B.C. Hydro litigation task force at the Hotel Georgia, which was located near the court house. The case was so complex that there were more than twenty-five lawyers from Bull, Housser and Tupper working on it, and they needed to rent space in the hotel for the lawyers and their books and files. Temporary storage cases had been erected there.

According to Bae Wallace, the lawyers in the case "had a 'war room' at the Hotel Georgia, where we . . . planned strategy, and dined and lunched and otherwise entertained ourselves in the Cavalier [bar/lounge/dining] Room." McLachlin arrived there just after lunch to meet the all-male group of lawyers she would be working with, and they were enjoying their post-lunch cigars. It occurred to Wallace that a young woman might be uncomfortable sitting around with cigar-smoking men, and so he asked if she minded if they continued with their cigars.

> She said, "Oh no; do you mind if I smoke?" And she
> pulled out one of those dark cigarillos. Right at the time,
> I thought, boy, she is making a statement. She is not
> going to be intimidated by cigar-smoking counsel, and
> she wasn't. She made a statement that impressed us all.
> But I've never seen her smoke since.[43]

The trial for the B.C. Hydro case was spread over three years. "We were working nights, days, weekends, but we really had a lot of fun,"[44] according to Wallace. About every three months, the lawyers' task force would have a retreat at resorts such as Harrison Hot Springs or Pasley Island in the Strait of Georgia, and they would bring their spouses with them

> because we certainly owed them the occasion to be with
> us and see us from time to time . . . and it was very much
> a team approach. And Beverley is perfect in that role —
> the way she handles the team work and generally makes
> the work ambience a pleasant one.[45]

As time went on, Bae Wallace became more and more impressed with the quality of McLachlin's work. On one occasion, he was preparing for a hearing at the Supreme Court of Canada, but the deadline for filing a factum in the B.C. Court of Appeal for another case was looming. He asked McLachlin to draft the Court of Appeal factum for him; he would read it on the plane and phone her from Ottawa with the changes he wanted.

> *I remember still sitting on that plane and turning over the pages of the factum that Beverley had drafted, and it was just exactly what I wanted to have. That only happens once in a lifetime: the pleasure of knowing, "this is exactly what I want," paragraph after paragraph, page after page. I got to Ottawa, and I got to the hotel and phoned up Beverley, and I said, "If you weren't married, I'd propose. That's a perfect factum; please go ahead and file it; there are no changes."* [46]

In 1974, McLachlin left Bull, Housser and Tupper to take up a position at the University of British Columbia law school, teaching civil litigation, but she continued to do part-time work for the firm.

THE UNIVERSITY OF BRITISH COLUMBIA

McLachlin commented that she had enjoyed the practice of law, "but I wanted to try teaching."[47] She liked teaching, and so applied for a tenure-track position, to which she was appointed in 1975.

This was a time when the university was wrestling with gender equity issues and the impact of the feminist movement.[48] There were lively debates on gender issues in every faculty; committees were struck, and reforms were undertaken. The first woman law faculty member in Canada had been appointed at UBC in 1955, but major changes to the curriculum regarding gender did not come until McLachlin's time on the faculty. For example,

> *Materials in the Evidence course at that time seemed to have been chosen according to the principle that, wherever possible, a given rule of evidence should be illustrated through a case involving rape, sexual assault,*

or some other humiliation of a woman . . . It was when
Beverley McLachlin . . . was a member of the law faculty
and undertook revisions of the Evidence materials that
they were changed.[49]

In addition, McLachlin developed UBC law school's first course
on women and the law.[50] But McLachlin had varied research
interests. In 1976, she assembled a comprehensive casebook on
consumer protection and began to put together a textbook on procedure and practice.[51]

With job security, McLachlin could contemplate having a child.
One of the women students in McLachlin's civil procedure class in
the spring term of 1976 commented that it was refreshing to take a
class with a young, outgoing and approachable woman law professor, who also happened to be pregnant.[52] McLachlin's son Angus
was born later in 1976. McLachlin was an inspirational contrast to
some of the older male professors, who occasionally made sexist
comments without even realizing it. She brought to life a rather
dry subject by making references to current popular culture. For
example, she said that instead of thinking about Paul Simon's "50
Ways to Leave Your Lover," think of fifty ways to settle a lawsuit.[53]

In 1977, McLachlin suffered another setback when her father,
who had remarried in 1974, died in July at the age of sixty-two.[54]
However, he lived long enough to see his daughter Beverley
become a law professor and his son Leonard become a medical
doctor, and to meet his grandson, Angus.

After recovering from losing her father and adjusting to moth-
erhood, McLachlin threw herself into her academic writing. She
enjoyed working with another faculty member, James Taylor,
and together they wrote *British Columbia Practice*,[55] which was
published in 1978. This book became a standard reference text
for B.C. lawyers and judges, and subsequent editions continued to
be published until after McLachlin was appointed to the Supreme
Court of Canada. She also began work with Bae Wallace on a book

about the law of architecture and engineering.[56] This book is a clearly written guide for architects and engineers about the legal principles that govern their work. It includes a concise guide to the Canadian legal system; the relationship between common law and statute law; ethical responsibilities to the public, the profession and clients; the impact of civil law for those practising in Quebec; and summaries of leading cases. Architects and engineers who read this book were more likely to respect their legal and ethical obligations and less likely to be subjected to lawsuits.

James Taylor remembered Beverley McLachlin as a collegial faculty member who stayed above petty university politics, promoted consensus and spoke her mind clearly:

> One of the things about Beverley as a colleague was that she had a very independent view of things. She reached her decisions quite independently of the rest of us. And she did it in a very creative way. I remember at faculty meetings, there was a group of people who didn't want to participate early on. Some of them put this down to high principle, but it was really a type of low politics — trying to get a steady idea of where the tide was before you chimed in with your points of view. That wasn't Beverley. Beverley would listen, and then she would take a position, and she would always become a part of the solution, and a part of the creation of a solution, instead of being just part of the coronation of an idea already adopted by the majority.[57]

As will be shown in later chapters, McLachlin adopted a similar approach in conferences with her colleagues at the Supreme Court of Canada, where she spoke her mind and encouraged other judges to do the same, with the expectation that they would take one another's viewpoints seriously and if possible, reach a consensus.

Taylor also remembered McLachlin as a staunchly loyal colleague. He recalled that after a discussion with a publisher about a potentially lucrative project, Taylor was unhappy about the terms of the proposal. McLachlin said without hesitation that she would back him up.[58]

BECOMING A JUDGE

McLachlin liked her career as an academic in the late 1970s and early 1980s, and enjoyed combining it with occasional litigation work for Bull, Housser and Tupper. She had never thought of becoming a judge until she was told by the chief justice of British Columbia that he had recommended her for a judgeship in 1981.[59]

As noted earlier, McLachlin enjoyed her work with Bae Wallace at Bull, Housser and Tupper. Wallace was appointed to the Supreme Court of British Columbia in 1979, the same year in which Allan McEachern, another leading Vancouver lawyer, was appointed chief justice of that same court. McEachern has described why he approached McLachlin to let her name stand as a County Court judge (the County Court, a local court that could hear some cases that would otherwise go to the Superior Court, was merged with the Superior Court in 1990):

In 1981 there was a vacancy on the County Court in Vancouver. There were no women on any of the County Courts at that time. The Minister of Justice was . . . Hon. Jean Chrétien. He told me to find the best qualified person to fill that vacancy on that court, but he added, "It better be a woman." I put down the phone, I went into the judges' lounge, where the trial judges met for coffee every morning . . . Bae Wallace . . . told me in no uncertain terms that Beverley McLachlin at UBC was the best possible candidate. I had complete confidence in Bae Wallace who was a great judge, a great lawyer . . . I phoned her, and we arranged to meet at a UBC

law faculty function that just happened to be on that
very evening. We met, and we talked, and I said that I
would recommend her appointment.[60]

McLachlin, however, was taken aback by McEachern's suggestion that she become a judge:

The government of the day was intent on getting more
women on the bench, and they were approaching chief
justices for names of women who could be appointed. I
had worked with one of the judges on the bench — Bae
Wallace — and also a little with the chief justice, Allan
McEachern. So Allan sidled up to me one day at a cock-
tail party and asked me if I'd like to be a judge. I said,
"Wow! I don't know about that!"[61]

McLachlin was hesitant about the offer of a judicial appointment. She was torn between thinking that a judgeship might be
an opportunity to advance the ideals she had championed as a law
professor, including the advancement of women in the ranks of
judges, and the fear that she would not like the job, and it would
turn out to be a dead end: "In those days, if you became a judge,
that was it, you stayed a judge."[62] The County Court position was
a junior position, "which was fine because I wasn't very senior and
I wasn't very old,"[63] but she worried that she might never be promoted to a more senior judgeship that would be more challenging
and engaging. Would she be able to accommodate her parenting
responsibilities with the same flexibility that her professorship
provided? After discussing the pros and cons with Rory and her
sister Judi (who also lived in Vancouver), "in the end, I took it, and
it worked out."[64]

McLachlin had had only a few months to adjust to the judicial
role in the County Court when a vacancy arose in the Supreme
Court of British Columbia, the province's superior-level trial court.

According to Chief Justice McEachern, "Five months later, I had the same conversation with the same minister of justice and with the same judge about a vacancy on the Supreme Court of British Columbia, and she [McLachlin] was quickly appointed to fill that vacancy."[65]

She served on the trial court until 1985, when a vacancy arose in the Supreme Court of British Columbia, the province's superior level trial court. Chief Justice McEachern recommended that McLachlin become the first woman to be appointed to the Court of Appeal, and Prime Minister Brian Mulroney made the appointment.[66] In 1986, Bae Wallace was promoted to the Court of Appeal and was delighted to be once again on the same court as Beverley McLachlin.[67] The next year was a difficult one for Beverley McLachlin because her husband, Rory, had been diagnosed with cancer. In 1988, Allan McEachern was appointed chief justice of the Court of Appeal, leaving a vacancy for that position on the B.C. Supreme Court. McEachern recommended McLachlin to replace him. Subsequently, Brian Mulroney appointed her to become the first woman chief justice of the Supreme Court of British Columbia. Sadly, Rory died a few days after her appointment.[68]

Among the many hundreds of decisions McLachlin contributed to during her eight years as a judge in British Columbia, two in particular stand out. The first was a decision that she wrote for the Court of Appeal in 1986, a year after being appointed to that court: *Andrews v. Law Society of British Columbia.*[69] Mark D. Andrews, who had moved to Canada from the United Kingdom, had fulfilled all requirements to become a practising lawyer in British Columbia, except that he did not meet the B.C. Law Society's requirement that he be a Canadian citizen. He had applied to become a citizen, but had to wait the required period. He claimed a violation of equality because of discrimination based on citizenship, arguing that citizenship was analogous to "national or ethnic origin," one of the prohibited grounds of discrimination in the *Charter*.

Andrews lost in the B.C. Supreme Court, where he initiated the case in 1985, but won in the B.C. Court of Appeal. McLachlin wrote that discriminatory laws or regulations that are unreasonable or unfair are prohibited by the *Charter*.[70] McLachlin's decision was upheld three years later by the Supreme Court of Canada, just two months prior to McLachlin's appointment to that court, though the top court adopted a broader definition of equality than McLachlin had employed.[71] The Supreme Court of Canada decision in *Andrews* was one of its most important regarding equality rights, discussed ahead.

The second decision was the *Dixon* case on electoral boundaries, which McLachlin decided in 1989 as chief justice of the Supreme Court of British Columbia.[72] McLachlin tackled the thorny issue of how much variation in the populations of electoral districts can be tolerated given the equality and democratic rights provisions of the *Charter*. She found that the B.C. legislation at that time, which allowed one riding to have fifteen times as many voters as another, was contrary to the *Charter*, but she left it to the legislature to find a remedy which would comply with the *Charter*. The *Dixon* decision laid the groundwork for the Supreme Court of Canada's first major decision on electoral boundaries in 1991[73] — a decision written by McLachlin, as discussed in the next chapter.

As others have commented, McLachlin rose through the judicial ranks more quickly than it takes most cases to go from trial to appeal to the Supreme Court of Canada.[74] In 1989, six months after she became chief justice of the B.C. Supreme Court, Brian Mulroney appointed her to the Supreme Court of Canada. Once again, he had a glowing recommendation from Chief Justice Allan McEachern, but McLachlin was also strongly recommended by Mulroney's political minister in B.C., John Fraser.[75] Beverley McLachlin became the third woman to be appointed to Canada's highest court, at the age of forty-six.[76] She was the youngest judge to have been appointed to the Supreme Court since 1940.[77]

McLachlin began her twenty-eight-year career on the Supreme Court as an associate justice. She brought with her the attributes that she honed from her time as an undergraduate at the University of Alberta through to her eight years as a Superior Court judge (both trial and appellate) in British Columbia. These qualities included increasingly clear and sharp writing skills, a love of the theory and practice of the rule of law, insistence on a thorough and sympathetic understanding of submissions and evidence, independent thinking and reasoning skills imbued with logic.

3

McLachlin on the Supreme Court: 1989–2000

Beverley McLachlin was appointed to the Supreme Court on March 30, 1989. This means that she joined the court right at the end of Brian Dickson's tenure as chief justice (1984–1990), so that her experience on the court before becoming chief justice herself was almost entirely during the chief justiceship of Antonio Lamer (1990–2000).

She was not the first woman to serve on the Supreme Court of Canada — Bertha Wilson from Ontario served on the court from 1982 to 1991, and Claire L'Heureux-Dubé from Quebec sat on the court from 1987 to 2002.[1] Given that Wilson retired early, less than two years after McLachlin joined the court, during most of her time as associate justice McLachlin had only one woman colleague.

IN THE BEGINNING

The Supreme Court of Canada consists of nine judges — a chief justice and eight associate justices.[2] The judges hear cases in panels of nine, seven or five, as determined by the chief justice. Cases that are considered to be the most important, from a legal or public perspective, are usually heard by nine judges. Sometimes this is not possible because, for example, a judge is not available or has a conflict of interest, and so a panel of seven is struck to avoid the potential for an evenly divided panel. Very occasionally, a judge will retire or have health issues, and the result is a decision-rendering panel of six or eight. Panels of five are used for Quebec civil law appeals, which always include the three judges from Quebec so that there will be a majority of judges trained in the civil law.[3] Five-judge panels are often used for as-of-right appeals[4] that do not raise significant legal or constitutional issues.

After a hearing, judges meet in a "conference" to present their views on what the outcome should be. The chief justice assigns one of the judges to write the first draft of what appears to be the consensus, or at least the majority opinion, of the court. The person selected is often the person who appears best to represent that consensus, or the person with the most expertise in that area of law, but it depends also on how many other cases that judge is currently writing. It is prudent for the chief justice to distribute the workload evenly.

It usually takes some time for a new appointee to begin writing his or her share of judgments; this time lag involves two separate elements. First, most Supreme Court decisions involve a "reserved" judgment, which is to say that after the parties have made their oral arguments before the court, the decision is not announced immediately but is "reserved" until the court has had time to write the (sometimes extended) reasons for judgment; this writing process includes a circulation for feedback from other judges. This time period is measured in months, averaging about five months under Dickson although sometimes it took much longer. Second, there is a transitional "socialization" element, as the new judge gets "up to speed" with respect to the procedures and expectations of the country's highest court, something which can be a little daunting even for experienced appeal court judges. This double delay normally means that a new Supreme Court judge delivers his or her first significant judgment about a year after appointment to the court. For example: Justice Sheilah Martin, who filled McLachlin's empty seat on the Court, was appointed on December 18, 2017, and handed down her first judgment for the court on December 14, 2018.[5]

McLachlin had a rather unusual debut on the court. She was appointed on March 30, 1989, and delivered her first judgment for the court in July — less than four months later.[6] Even more striking was the cluster of no fewer than six judgments that she wrote for the court in September of that year, followed by the lead majority judgment for a badly divided panel in early October involving a constitutional case (*MacKeigan v. Hickman*, discussed below), in which the central issue was significant — the independence of the judiciary.[7]

PARTICIPATION AS ASSOCIATE JUSTICE

The distinctive feature of McLachlin's participation on the Lamer court was not the number of judgments she wrote but rather the frequency with which she wrote to distinguish herself from the judgment-delivering majority. In the decade of the Lamer Court, she wrote seventy-eight judgments of all kinds but a total of 115 sets of separate reasons (fifty-eight dissents and fifty-seven separate concurrences).[8] Only L'Heureux-Dubé (with seventy-four dissents and sixty-nine separate concurrences, against sixty-three judgments) did so proportionately more often. Part of the context of these numbers is that the Lamer Court divided rather frequently, to the extent that later on as chief justice, McLachlin made it her mission to lead a more united Court. Another reason might be that McLachlin perhaps did not enjoy the same positive relationship with Chief Justice Lamer that she had briefly enjoyed with Dickson.

The central vote-counting logic of the Lamer Court (and as many Supreme Court judges in this and other countries candidly observe, counting votes is the pragmatic underlying reality as judges engage with the issues in any appeal decision) was the "gang of five."[9] There was a general tendency, verified by factual analysis, for an identifiable five judges to form the core of many of the court's major judgments, on the basis of unusually high "two-judge agreement rates" for all ten of the pairings within that five-judge group. Those five judges were Chief Justice Lamer, John Major, John Sopinka, Frank Iacobucci and Peter Cory. This was not as monolithic and totally predictable a bloc as, for example, the groups within the United States Supreme Court in recent years, and there were both occasional "defections" from the group (especially by Cory) and many cases in which one or more of the "non-gang" judges signed on.

If "gang of five" is a slightly-too-casual label for the majority, a closer examination shows that this group was not confronted by a comparably solid "gang of four" in opposition but rather by a "gang of two" (Gérard La Forest and Charles Gonthier) with two outliers, those being L'Heureux-Dubé and McLachlin. That is to say: the central mathematical logic of the Lamer Court was not "5–4" but rather "5–2–1–1," with L'Heureux-Dubé and McLachlin being the "1"s. L'Heureux-Dubé was the one who gained the reputation of being the Court's maverick — her minority reasons were slightly more frequent, typically much longer and often more dramatic and colourful.[10] McLachlin and L'Heureux-Dubé were frequently in the minority on the same case, often voting the same way but usually writing separately rather than signing on to a single set of reasons, even if their central arguments seemed to be following somewhat similar tracks.

This analysis suggests an enhanced incentive for some judges to write minority reasons. If the judgment delivery process tends to be dominated by a certain subset of the court, in such a way that the less senior judges get squeezed out of that part of the process even when they are trying to suggest that the majority is overlooking some important aspects to the resolution of the issue,[11] then the only way to have voice into the law is to write separately. Having voice is why judges want to serve on the Court in the first place.

Elliot Slotnick (working from data from the United States Supreme Court) has suggested something of a vicious circle here. If a judge disagrees — and writes minority reasons — frequently, this tends to generate a degree of resentment on the part of their majority colleagues, with the result that they will not get "their share" of judgments to write even when they are "onside."[12] If you cannot influence from the centre, then you are obliged to influence from the margins. We believe that ultimately, McLachlin as chief justice devised a strategy to resolve this conundrum of whether to join or dissent, with considerable success.

On the Lamer Court (compared with the Laskin and Dickson Courts that preceded it, and the McLachlin Court that followed it), additional reasons for dissent existed, largely due to the unusual imperative of interpreting a newly entrenched *Charter of Rights*. The most obvious and understandable reason to be writing in dissent stems from a feeling that "the majority got it wrong." However, the other type of disagreement results in a separate concurrence, which means agreeing with the outcome but disagreeing with the reasons. This is important because the function of an appeal court is not simply to declare a winner but to state the law that explains that outcome.

Even if you think the majority reached the right decision, you could have a different sense of the framing of the issue and of the relevant portions of established law that best help to explain the outcome, and these differences will carry forward-reaching precedential implications. Minority reasons are not just "loser's history," and certainly not error in any simple sense. Functionally, they are an assurance to the losing side that they were listened to; they are a signal to potential litigants that some judges are ready to listen if they come up with appealing cases and strong arguments, and they are a way to put ideas "in play" for future majorities to accommodate, even to follow.

Minority reasons are far from being wasted words. On the Lamer Court, about one in every nine of the court's citations of its own previous decisions involved citing a set of minority reasons, suggesting the actual practice of precedent in Canada is a little more flexible than the most literal understanding of stare decisis — the doctrine that judges must follow precedents — might suggest.[13] L'Heureux-Dubé's impact on equality rights under the *Charter* through her minority decisions is an excellent example of gradual "water on stone" influence in that, not infrequently, her dissents eventually became the majority view. Some of McLachlin's leading dissents had a similar impact.

Following are commentaries on several of McLachlin's decisions — both majority or minority — that illustrate her reasoning and her strategies in tackling a number of issues of importance to Canadians during her time as associate justice. The touchstones of McLachlin's approach to decision-making are the rule of law, a thorough, impartial and sympathetic canvassing of submissions by the parties — what she has referred to as "conscious objectivity" — and reliance on sound evidence.

With regard to the rule of law, the preamble to the *Constitution Act, 1982* states that "Canada is founded upon principles that recognize the supremacy of God[14] and the rule of law." The rule of law has a long history in common law. It refers to a system of government according to the laws of legitimate law-makers rather than arbitrary decree, and the equal application of the law. In the Supreme Court's decision in the *Quebec Secession Reference*, which McLachlin helped to write, the court stated that "the rule of law vouchsafes to the citizens and residents of the country a stable, predictable and ordered society . . . It provides a shield for individuals from arbitrary state action."[15] The court outlined three basic attributes of the rule of law: "The law is supreme over the acts of both government and private persons," there is "an actual order of positive laws" and "the relationship between the state and the individual must be regulated by law."[16]

The law is not always clear, and so judges develop interpretive approaches. In a 2015 interview, McLachlin stated,

What you have to try to do as a judge . . . whether you're on Charter *issues or any other issue, is by an act of the imagination put yourself in the shoes of the different parties, and think about how it looks from their perspective, and really think about it, not just give it lip service.*[17]

She describes this process as "conscious objectivity" — the second touchstone of her decision-making approach. Trying to put yourself in someone else's shoes might also be referred to as empathy.

McLachlin's third touchstone — reliance on sound evidence — runs throughout her decisions. Perhaps because of her background in philosophy and academia, she is skilled in distinguishing strong and reliable evidence from evidence that is not so dependable.

These three attributes characterize McLachlin's decisions as associate justice on the Supreme Court as well as her decisions later on as chief justice. McLachlin arrived at the Supreme Court during one of its most tumultuous periods. The typical 5–2–1–1 division of judges, described above, demonstrated much more than intellectual disagreement. According to a retired Supreme Court judge, "It was crazy then . . . There was permanent conflict. There was no common sense."[18]

There was particular animosity between Chief Justice Lamer and Justice Claire L'Heureux-Dubé that sometimes led to shouting matches when the judges conferenced after a hearing.[19] These displays of temper were distressing to McLachlin, and both through her social interaction with other judges and in the way she wrote her opinions, she tried to lower the temperature without compromising her jurisprudential principles.[20]

JUDICIAL INDEPENDENCE

Only six months after joining the Supreme Court, McLachlin wrote the main judgment for a divided court in *MacKeigan v. Hickman* about judicial immunity from testimony.[21] This was a highly unusual development in at least three respects. First, the judgment was written by the most junior member of the court when she was only six months into her tenure.[22] Second, this was a significant case involving constitutional issues.[23] Third, McLachlin was assigned the writing of the judgment despite the reservations of her more senior colleagues (including the Chief Justice, who formally makes the assignment), even though the hearing took place less than a month after she was appointed to the court.

As background to this case, Donald Marshall Jr. had been convicted of murder in 1971, but was eventually acquitted by the Nova Scotia Court of Appeal in 1983. The Court of Appeal panel that acquitted Marshall included Justice Leonard Pace, who had been the attorney general of Nova Scotia when Marshall was wrongfully convicted. The panel wrote that Marshall was in large part the author of his own misfortunes. Both the fact that Pace had been assigned to the panel — an obvious conflict of interest — and the panel's unwise comment about Marshall led the Nova Scotia government to appoint a royal commission of inquiry headed by two superior court judges and one retired judge from other provinces.[24]

The commission wanted members of the Court of Appeal to testify before it both about the mechanics of how the panel that acquitted Marshall was struck and the evidence that supported the panel's comment about Marshall's role in his wrongful conviction. Chief Justice Ian MacKeigan of the Nova Scotia Court of Appeal objected to the appearance of the judges before the inquiry, citing judicial immunity, and that objection went all the way to the Supreme Court for determination.

Marshall's mistreatment and the commission's inquiry were major news items across Canada at the time, and it is an indication of McLachlin's courage and ability to navigate her way through troubled waters that she ended up writing the main decision for the Court. Her decision declared that to protect judicial independence, judges are immune from having to testify about how they make their decisions or how panels of judges are struck by the chief justice. McLachlin's decision, which Gonthier and L'Heureux-Dubé signed on to, summarizes the history of the principle of judicial independence as a support for judicial impartiality, and the necessity for such impartiality in a rule-of-law country. The decision is clear, logical and unequivocal. Two judges, Lamer and La Forest, wrote their own less detailed reasons in support of judicial immunity, while Wilson and Cory would have allowed limited exceptions to judicial immunity in extraordinary circumstances such as this one. McLachlin's decision in *MacKeigan v. Hickman* displays intellectual leadership on a significant issue from the most junior judge. We have never seen a junior judge on the Supreme Court take a leadership role so decisively and quickly before or since. The decision also illustrates the fractured nature of the Court during the 1990s, including the judges' divided approach to fundamental principles such as judicial independence. It was not until McLachlin became chief justice that the Court became unified in its reasoning about the scope and application of judicial independence.[25]

ELECTORAL DEMOCRACY

Electoral Boundaries (1991)

McLachlin had been on the Supreme Court for only two years when she wrote the majority decision in a case about setting electoral boundaries for provincial elections in Saskatchewan.[26] It should be noted that McLachlin had experience with the issue of electoral boundaries and constituency sizes from her time as chief justice of the Superior Court in British Columbia. Her decision in the *Dixon* case (from that period) found that it was a violation of section 3 of the *Charter* (the right to vote) for one constituency to have fifteen times the population of another, and that this discrepancy could not be justified as a reasonable limit under section 1 of the *Charter*.[27] Up to that time, this was one of the most important court decisions on electoral boundaries any-where in Canada.[28]

In the Saskatchewan case, the central issue was how much deviance from equality of population in electoral districts could be allowed for the result to be considered "democratic." Perfect mathematical equality is impossible. The issue was what deviation from perfect equality is acceptable to comply with section 3 of the *Charter of Rights*, which stipulates that "every citizen has the right to vote." The *Charter*'s stipulation that "every individual is equal" is also relevant.

McLachlin's analysis was both pragmatic and evidence-based. The Saskatchewan government of Premier Grant Devine had enacted legislation that changed the rules by which the Saskatchewan Electoral Boundaries Commission could redraw the boundaries of electoral districts for the upcoming provincial election, giving the commission more latitude in redrawing the boundaries than earlier legislation. For example, the commission could create constituencies with up to a 25 per cent deviation from the average constituency population, instead of the previous limit of up to 15 per cent.[29] Some people were concerned that the new legislation might result in the kind of "gerrymandering" of boundaries that occurs in some parts of the United States, allowing those in government to retain their power because the commission would concentrate opposition supporters in specific areas in order to dilute their voting impact.

In this case, McLachlin deferred to the will of the Saskatchewan legislature. However, the importance of her decision was her inter-pretation of section 3 of the *Charter* as guaranteeing "effective representation." She noted that to ensure effective representation, in addition to requiring relatively equal populations from riding to riding, "factors like geography, community history, commu-nity interests and minority representation may need to be taken into account to ensure that our legislative assemblies effectively represent the diversity of our social mosaic."[30] She conducted an

extensive review of the evidence about the impact of the new legislation, and concluded that the distribution of voters by the Electoral
Boundaries Commission was about the same as under the old legislation. Seldom did the deviation approach the upper limit, and
there were good reasons for deviations. The decision suggested that
future courts would not tolerate arbitrary decisions about changes
to electoral boundaries that could be considered gerrymandering.

Thanks to this decision, any attempts to gerrymander electoral
boundaries in Canada would be unconstitutional. McLachlin
found a way to defer to the Saskatchewan legislature and at the
same time set limits on the discretion of electoral boundaries commissions to ensure a reasonable equality of populations in electoral
districts. Nevertheless, the court was divided, with Sopinka writing
a separate concurring decision, and Lamer, L'Heureux-Dubé and
Cory dissenting. The dissenters wrote that the discretion given
by the legislation to the commission was itself a violation of the
Charter, and declaring of a *Charter* violation would send a stronger
signal to governments tempted to gerrymander than the declaration of principles in McLachlin's decision. Perhaps as a vindication
of McLachlin's decision, the scandal-ridden party of Grant Devine
was defeated in the subsequent provincial election; the new electoral boundaries had no impact on diminishing the magnitude of
the government's defeat.[31]

Quebec Secession Reference (1998)

In 1995, voters in Quebec narrowly defeated separation from Canada in a referendum question. The pro-sovereignty government
of Jacques Parizeau had claimed that, had their pro-independence
referendum been won by 50 per cent plus one votes, the Quebec
government could have unilaterally declared the independence of
Quebec, and the government had plans to do so. Under both Canadian and international law, this claim was questionable.

To refute the Parizeau government's claims, in 1996 the federal government of Jean Chrétien sent a reference question to the

Supreme Court requesting an opinion about the legality of the secession of a province. Hearings were held in early 1998, and the Court released its decision in August of that year. No doubt, the Chrétien government expected a short decision simply stating that Quebec could not unilaterally secede from Canada under either Canadian or international law. The Court did affirm this conclusion, but it did so via a ninety-page decision outlining the fundamental principles of Canadian democracy and, given these principles, the steps necessary for a province to secede. Perhaps the judges contemplated a future scenario in which a province voted to secede in a referendum, and it wanted to minimize chaos by outlining the legal steps necessary for valid secession.

The decision was by "The Court." All nine judges participated in the decision: Chief Justice Lamer, Claire L'Heureux-Dubé, Charles Gonthier, Peter Cory, Beverley McLachlin, Frank Iacobucci, John Major, Michel Bastarache and Ian Binnie. But it is clear that McLachlin played a major part in discussions among the judges about how to answer the reference question, and in drafting the decision.[32] When we asked McLachlin about her "favourite" decisions, she mentioned that "the secession reference truly took us into new areas and new concerns, was very very challenging, but a challenge I think the Court by and large met for the country. So it's a highlight."[33]

In 2003, McLachlin remarked that when the judges were working out their response to the reference question, "Everybody had to collaborate. It was a real collaborative effort in the true sense. Everybody talked, everybody listened while we worked out what we could say about these profoundly difficult questions that would be true to the Constitution."[34]

The Court declared that "four foundational constitutional principles . . . are most germane for resolution of this Reference: federalism, democracy, constitutionalism and the rule of law, and respect for minority rights,"[35] all linked to one another in a mutually reinforcing relationship: "The principles are not merely descriptive, but are also invested with a powerful normative force, and are binding upon both courts and governments."[36]

Starting with federalism, the Court noted that "the principle of federalism recognizes the diversity of the component parts of Confederation, and the autonomy of provincial governments to develop their societies within their respective spheres of jurisdiction."[37] Referring to McLachlin's decision in the *Saskatchewan Electoral Boundaries Reference*, the Court pointed out that the Canadian tradition is "one of evolutionary democracy moving in uneven steps toward the goal of universal suffrage and more effective representation."[38] Democracy is more than a system of government by majority rule. Again, referring to the *Saskatchewan Reference*, the court emphasized that democracy is concerned more with substantive goals rather than mere process, foremost among them the promotion of self-government that "accommodates cultural and group identities."[39]

A successful democracy can only thrive within the context of the rule of law and respectful discussion:

> *The need to build majorities necessitates compromise, negotiation and deliberation. No one has a monopoly on truth, and our system is predicated on the faith that in the marketplace of ideas, the best solutions to public problems will rise to the top. Inevitably, there will be dissenting voices. A democratic system of government is committed to considering those dissenting voices, and seeking to acknowledge and address those voices in the laws by which all in the community must live.*[40]

Thus, the duty of democratic discussion must "acknowledge and address democratic expressions of a desire for change in other provinces."[41]

The Court's description of the rule of law was summarized at the beginning of this chapter. Constitutionalism is related to the rule of law in that all orders of government in Canada are bound both by the rule of law and by the Constitution. The Constitution can be amended, "but only through a process of negotiation which ensures that there is an opportunity for the constitutionally defined rights of all the parties to be respected and reconciled."[42]

Respect for minority rights is a long-held Canadian tradition, beginning with the guarantees of minority language, education and religious rights built into the 1867 Constitution, and continuing with the carefully thought-out minority rights protections in the Canadian *Charter of Rights and Freedoms*. The protection of minority rights is fundamental to the existence of Canada.[43]

Building on these principles, the Court ruled that a referendum with a "clear question" that demonstrated a "clear majority" in favour of secession would place the onus on the rest of Canada to negotiate a change in the constitutional order. The meaning of a "clear question" and a "clear majority" would be determined by the political process. On a more critical note, the Court had gone beyond the questions posed to it about whether Quebec had a right to secede under either existing Canadian or international law to answer the different question of how Quebec could go about seceding; only time will tell how significant this concession will be.

By writing a decision based on carefully reasoned principles about the broad nature of democracy, the judges' intent was to create a platform for peaceful and ordered advancement in case any future referendum on secession produced a Yes result. Both the federal and Quebec governments subsequently enacted contradictory resolutions addressing the nature of a clear question and a clear majority. Nevertheless, the Supreme Court's decision seems to have contributed to lowering the temperature over the secession debate.

HATE SPEECH CASES (1990 AND 1992)
One of the hardest decisions Canadian judges have had to make is about the constitutionality of legislation intended to prevent hate

speech. On one hand, the *Charter of Rights* protects freedom of expression. On the other hand, in a free and democratic society, everyone is equally deserving of respect and dignity.

McLachlin believed that the use of the *Criminal Code* to punish hate speech does more harm than good. However, she noted, "Discrimination on grounds of race and religion is worthy of suppression. Human rights legislation, focusing on reparation rather than punishment, has had considerable success in discouraging such conduct."[44]

During the 1960s, there was an upsurge in racist propaganda directed at Blacks and Jews in parts of Canada. In response, Parliament commissioned a comprehensive study of the problem and enacted Canada's anti–hate speech law.[45] James Keegstra was a high school teacher in a small Alberta town in the 1970s. He taught his students that the Holocaust was a hoax and that Jews were evil. To pass their exams, students had to write in agreement with Keegstra's teachings. In 1983, Keegstra was charged with violating the anti–hate speech law, and his case reached the Supreme Court of Canada in 1990.[46] Given the difficulty of the issues in the case, the seven-judge panel was split four to three. The majority decision of Chief Justice Dickson upheld the hate speech law. Beverley McLachlin wrote a dissenting opinion supported by two other judges; her central point was that the *Charter* protects the conveying of a meaning or message through non-violent expression, no matter how offensive the message might be, and nothing in Keegstra's teaching directly advocated violence. She further suggested that a harmful effect of the law was that it attracted a great deal of free publicity for Keegstra; the law might have a chilling effect on legitimate speech; and the best way to combat hate speech is to confront it through free expression and human rights commissions, not through criminal sanctions.[47]

Although McLachlin's reasons in *Keegstra* were written in dissent, in 1992 another Holocaust denier ended up in the Supreme Court, and this time McLachlin wrote the majority decision.[48]

Ernst Zundel immigrated to Canada from Germany in 1958, and until 1985 distributed literature denying the Holocaust and denigrating Jews. He could have been charged under the anti–hate speech section of the *Criminal Code*, and likely would have been convicted, given the Supreme Court's decision in *Keegstra*. However, he was charged under a much older part of the *Criminal Code* — spreading false news.

Canada's original *Criminal Code* was a codification of English criminal law. "Spreading false news" was an English law dating from 1275, whose purpose was to protect the reputation of the aristocracy. It likely ended up in Canada's *Criminal Code* by accident, as it had already been repealed in England. At the Supreme Court, McLachlin wrote the majority decision striking down the "spreading false news" section of the *Criminal Code*. Her argument was similar to the one she wrote in the *Keegstra* case — but in addition, she wrote that this section of the *Criminal Code* was outdated. Although Zundel won his case, he was eventually deported to Germany and ended up in jail.[49]

McLachlin's contention that human rights commissions are a more effective way to tackle hate speech than the *Criminal Code* was vindicated in a 1996 decision. Malcolm Ross was a school teacher in New Brunswick from the 1970s to the 1990s. Like Keegstra and Zundel, Ross was anti-Jewish, and used the media to spread his views. Although he did not advance his anti-Semitic views in the classroom, his school board was ordered by the Human Rights Commission to take Ross out of the classroom because his well-known views were inappropriate considering the vulnerable population of school children. Ross appealed all the way to the Supreme Court and lost. The unanimous decision of the full court was written by the court's New Brunswick judge, La Forest.[50] McLachlin was part of that decision.

LEGAL RIGHTS DECISIONS

Sexual Assault: *Seaboyer* (1991)

Sexual assault is a serious offence. Most victims are women. In 1983, the Canadian Parliament enacted new *Criminal Code* provisions that severely restricted people accused of sexual assault from obtaining evidence about an alleged victim's prior sexual history. These provisions became known as "rape shield" provisions. Before the 1983 legislation, it was common for lawyers defending those accused of sexual assault to question victims about their prior sexual relationships in case they could use that evidence to encourage judges or juries to consider the alleged victim promiscuous, and to suggest that the alleged perpetrator was simply participating in consensual sex. Of course, this practice meant that many sexual assault victims would refuse to report a sexual assault or, if they did, would refuse to testify because of how they would be treated.

The rape shield legislation of 1983 was challenged at trial by lawyers representing men accused of sexual assault, and the issue reached the Supreme Court in 1991 in the *Seaboyer* case.[51] By this time, several democracies had enacted legislation similar to Canada's 1983 rape shield law. All nine judges on the Supreme Court participated in the *Seaboyer* decision, and Beverley McLachlin wrote the decision for the majority of seven.[52]

She reviewed various approaches that had been used to prevent unnecessary intrusion into the privacy of sexual assault victims, and concluded that Canada's was among the strictest. Canada's 1983 legislation left open the possibility that trial judges could occasionally admit evidence of the complainant's previous sexual history, but only in extremely limited circumstances. McLachlin wrote that these circumstances were more restrictive than necessary, and parts of the 1983 legislation violated the right to a fair hearing, in that the ability to make a "full answer and defence" was unnecessarily restricted. Her majority decision ordered Seaboyer back to trial under rules that might allow the trial judge to admit evidence of parts of the complainant's prior sexual history, if relevant.

L'Heureux-Dubé penned a critical minority decision, supported by Gonthier. L'Heureux-Dubé argued that the prior sexual history of the complainant is almost never relevant in a sexual assault trial, and arguments supporting its relevance are based on myths and stereotypes.[53] However, McLachlin's approach to the rule of law led her to come to a different conclusion, one that required a fair hearing for all, including those accused of sexual assault, in addition to a regime that protected the victims of sexual assault from unnecessary intrusions into their privacy. Feminist legal commentary was nearly unanimously on the side of L'Heureux-Dubé. For example, Professor Martha Shafer wrote that "Madam Justice McLachlin has now opened the door for men accused of sexual assault to attempt to convince the court that they thought the complainant was consenting based on what they 'knew' about her 'sexual proclivities.'"[54]

In 1992, Parliament re-enacted the rape shield law with provisions that took into account McLachlin's critique, but which in other ways provided even more protection for the privacy of sexual assault victims. When this new legislation reached the Supreme Court shortly after McLachlin became chief justice, it was upheld by a unanimous court as having achieved a fair balance between the right to a fair trial and victims' right to privacy.[55]

Assisted Dying: *Rodriguez* (1993)

In 1993, the Supreme Court for the first time considered the constitutionality of the *Criminal Code*'s prohibition of doctor-assisted suicide for those at the ends of their lives.[56] Sue Rodriguez was a forty-two-year-old woman suffering from amyotrophic lateral sclerosis (Lou Gehrig's disease). The court was split five to four on the outcome, with four different sets of reasons. The majority upheld the prohibition on assisted suicide, in part because of concerns that there would be inadequate protections for vulnerable individuals, such as the mentally handicapped. In dissent, McLachlin and L'Heureux-Dubé argued that the prohibition "deprives Sue Rodriguez of her security of the person (the right to make decisions concerning her own body, which affect only her own body) in a way that offends the principles of fundamental justice, thereby violating s. 7 of the *Charter*."[57]

McLachlin told us that her dissent in *Rodriguez* was one of her "highlight dissents."[58] It paved the way for the *Carter* decision of 2015, which removed the criminal penalty from doctor-assisted suicide.

EQUALITY RIGHTS

McLachlin did not join the Supreme Court until two months after its first decision on the meaning of section 15 —equality rights —was made in the *Andrews* decision of 1989.[59] In this case, the Court was considering an appeal by the Law Society of British Columbia of a decision written by McLachlin in 1986 as chief justice of the B.C. Court of Appeal (see previous chapter).

In *Andrews*, the Supreme Court essentially upheld the 1986 decision, but adopted a substantive equality approach, in which all "human beings [are] equally deserving of concern, respect, and consideration."[60] Inequality exists where the law or public officials discriminate on the basis of personal characteristics, not an individual's merits or capacities. These personal characteristics include those listed in section 15 — race, national or ethnic origin, colour, religion, sex, age and mental or physical disability — and categories analogous to these (such as citizenship and, in later cases, sexual orientation). People in these categories are considered discriminated against if they were denied benefits provided to others or were subjected to disadvantages that others were not exposed to. If discrimination is established according to the evidence, then there is a *Charter* violation unless the government can prove that the discrimination constitutes a reasonable limit in the democratic context.

In the mid-1990s, the Court decided two important equality cases involving claims of discrimination based on sex. In both these cases, McLachlin and L'Heureux-Dubé dissented. In the *Symes* decision of 1993, McLachlin and L'Heureux-Dubé would have allowed Elizabeth Symes, a partner in a law firm, to deduct the full cost of her nanny's wages in the calculation of her income tax so that she could continue in her career.[61] In the *Thibaudeau* case of 1995, McLachlin and L'Heureux-Dubé would have allowed divorced custodial parents (98 per cent of whom were women) to deduct child support alimony from their income for tax purposes.[62]

With regard to cases involving same-sex rights, McLachlin wrote consistently in support of equality rights for same-sex couples in cases decided in 1995 and 1998.[63] By this time, it seemed that interpretation of equality rights was so complex that clarification about how the *Andrews* decision would be applied was necessary. In 1999, the *Andrews* decision was supplemented in a unanimous court decision by a seven-judge panel written by Iacobucci in a case known as *Law*.[64] McLachlin signed on to Iacobucci's opinion, which over time turned out to be an overly complex test for equality compared with *Andrews*. As chief justice, she helped the Court retreat from the unnecessary complexities in *Law*. Her life experience had taught her to take the time necessary to make what appears to be the right decision but, if it appears that a mistake has been made, to admit it and move on.[65]

RIGHTS OF INDIGENOUS PEOPLES

As an associate justice on the Supreme Court, McLachlin regularly signed on to decisions that advanced First Nations' claims to uphold their treaty rights and land claims in areas not covered by treaties. As well, she dissented when she concluded that the majority had been either too restrictive or too deferential to Indigenous peoples. Later on, as chief justice, she wrote decisions that advanced First Nations' claims. McLachlin has expressed the opinion that in coming years, it is the issue of reconciliation with First Nations that will define the Supreme Court more than the *Charter of Rights*.[66]

Van der Peet Dissent (1996)

In 1973, the Supreme Court's decision in *Calder*[67] opened the door
to confirming that the Indigenous peoples of Canada have legitimate claims to lands that they occupied prior to treaty settlements,
including land concerning which treaties had never been negotiated. During the negotiations that led to the *Charter of Rights* and
the new amending formula for the Canadian Constitution in 1982,
Indigenous peoples insisted that their rights be included in the
updated constitution. The result was the inclusion of section 35
in the *Constitution Act, 1982*: "The existing aboriginal and treaty
rights of the aboriginal peoples of Canada are hereby recognized
and affirmed."[68] In 1990, in the *Sparrow* decision, the Supreme
Court declared that section 35 should be interpreted in a purposive
and liberal way.[69]

The first major Indigenous case that McLachlin participated in
on the Supreme Court was *Van der Peet*, in 1996.[70] The issue was
whether members of the Sto:lo band, fishing with an Indian food
fish licence issued under Canada's *Fisheries Act*, could sell some
of the fish they caught outside the band. Lamer wrote the majority
decision, in which he affirmed that evidence from Indigenous traditional sources must be given proper weight. However, he wrote that
Indigenous activities protected by section 35 are those existing prior
to European contact, and his view was that bartering fish with other
tribes or peoples was not part of pre-European practice for the Sto:lo.

McLachlin wrote a dissenting opinion. Her conclusion about the
evidence was that the right of the Sto:lo to sell fish was protected
by section 35 as part of their tradition, and as a reasonable modern
application of their historic use of the resources of river and sea to
sustain themselves. She concluded that this right still existed, and
so she would have ruled in favour of *Van der Peet*.[71]

Delgamuukw (1997)[72]

The *Calder* decision of 1973 opened the door for Indigenous
peoples to negotiate land claims settlements in vast areas of

Canada where there had been no treaties signed. Frank Calder was a chief of the Nisga'a Nation in central British Columbia. Even after the Supreme Court decision in *Calder*, the federal and provincial governments were resistant to negotiating a land claims settlement with the Nisga'a or any other First Nations. The inclusion of section 35 in the constitution in 1982 gave First Nations peoples the basis for bringing suits to court, which the Gitxsan and Wet'suwet'en peoples of British Columbia, neighbours of the Nisga'a, did in 1984.[73]

From 1984, there was a combination of litigation and unsuccessful negotiation before the Gitxsan and Wet'suwet'en litigation reached the Supreme Court in the mid-1990s in a case known as *Delgamuukw*. The main decision was written by Chief Justice Lamer and concurred in by McLachlin, Cory and Major.[74] The decision held that the trial judge had not given enough weight to evidence from traditional Indigenous sources. The case was sent back for retrial under the new evidentiary requirements, along with a set of general principles for land claims settlements. Both the summary of the evidentiary rules and the general principles for settlements indicate McLachlin's influence in terms of the affirmation of Aboriginal rights, and seem to echo her approach in the *Van der Peet* dissent. The *Delgamuukw* decision set the stage for the Nisga'a treaty in 2000, the first modern land claims settlement in British Columbia.[75]

Marshall Dissent (1999)[76]

In the *Marshall* case of 1999, McLachlin wrote a dissent, concurred in by Gonthier, in which she interpreted a Mi'kmaw treaty right more narrowly than the majority. In her dissent, she emphasized evidence and the rule of law. Although in previous decisions she had outlined the discrimination against First Nations in Canada's history, she wrote that was not a good enough reason for her to interpret treaty rights more broadly than she thought was intended.

The issue in the Marshall case was whether treaties signed

between the Mi'kmaq and the British in 1760 and 1761 should take precedence over federal fishing regulations. The case was brought to court by Donald Marshall Jr. — the same person who had been wrongfully convicted of murder in Nova Scotia in 1971 and, as already noted, was the focus of the first Supreme Court decision written by McLachlin, *MacKeigan v. Hickman*.[77]

In the 1760s, the British had been anxious to win the support of Indigenous peoples in the Maritimes. The British had defeated the French at Louisbourg in 1758; at the time, the Mi'kmaq had been allied with the French. The treaties gave the Mi'kmaq the right to trade products of hunting, fishing and gathering exclusively with the British. The outcome of the case depended on evidence about the Indigenous understanding of the treaties. Although the treaties were supplemented by licensed traders in 1762, the majority of five on the Supreme Court's seven-judge panel ruled that the 1760 and 1762 treaties were still in effect, and gave the Mi'kmaq the right to fish to earn a "moderate livelihood."[78]

On the other hand, McLachlin's analysis of the evidence was that the 1760–1762 treaties constituted a temporary measure after the fall of Louisbourg, and that by the 1780s the system established by the treaties had been replaced with new procedures. These changes eventually led to the Mi'kmaq being subject to the same rules of commerce as everyone else.[79]

The Supreme Court's decision, released on September 18, 1999, led to instant chaos in some fishing communities in the Maritimes. Some Indigenous fishers interpreted the decision as the right to ignore federal fishing regulations. Their fishing activities in disregard of the federal regulations angered non-Indigenous fishers to the point of violence.[80] Non-Indigenous fishers were so incensed that they applied for a rehearing of the decision. In an unusual move, the Supreme Court heard arguments for a rehearing, but then denied the application in a written decision on November 17.[81] In the decision to deny the rehearing, the Supreme Court emphasized the parts of its September 18 decision that upheld the right of the federal government to make regulations to protect fisheries for the benefit of all fishers, Indigenous and non-Indigenous.

A differently worded decision in September might have prevented the violence. Perhaps McLachlin realized the inflammatory situation regarding fisheries in the Maritimes, and her dissent was an attempt to encourage cooler heads to prevail. But McLachlin was still an associate judge with limited ability to encourage the other judges to consider alternative perspectives.[82]

McLachlin signed on to the "By The Court" decision of the November 17 rehearing decision. Being part of the decision by "The Court," McLachlin would have had some influence in the wording of the November 17 decision, which emphasized that the federal government's regulatory role was still in effect. It took a decade after the two Marshall decisions for the fisheries situation in the Maritimes to normalize. Indigenous fishers won more respect, and government regulations were redrafted to better consider the long-term needs of all fishers.[83]

McLACHLIN'S IMPACT AS ASSOCIATE JUSTICE

Beverley McLachlin jumped in to the decision-writing process within a few months of her appointment to the Supreme Court in 1989. Her well-organized, no-nonsense style, which was grounded consistently in the rule of law, strong evidence and conscious objectivity, would have been a breath of fresh air for the Court in its fractured state.

In the mid-1990s, Ian Greene interviewed eight of the nine judges on the Supreme Court for a research project.[84] His impression was that some judges, other than McLachlin, L'Heureux-Dubé and Sopinka, appeared tired and stressed. Given her relative youth and her enthusiasm for the work, McLachlin became a steadying force, helping to clarify the Court's jurisprudence and to move it forward progressively on issues such as judicial independence, electoral democracy, freedom of speech, legal and equality rights and the rights of Indigenous peoples.

Part way through McLachlin's decade as Associate Justice, in 1992, she married again. In our interview with her, McLachlin described to us how she met Frank McArdle, a lawyer who ran a legal conference for Canadians held every second year at the University of Cambridge:

> *After I became Chief Justice of British Columbia, [Frank] came to the court asking whether I, as Chief Justice, could continue doing something that my predecessors had done, which was give some assistance to a seminar the Canadian Institute for Advanced Legal Studies was running at the time in Stanford.... That's when I first got to know him. And then in the next summer, in 1989, I went to the Cambridge Lectures, and Frank was still involved in running them. I got to know him a little better. I was a widow by then, and took my thirteen-year-old son Angus with me, and Frank was very good at looking after my son. The next year we got to know each other a little better. I stopped in to see him in Toronto because he asked me to, and Angus wanted to see him. And eventually we started seeing each other. And as everyone knows, he proposed to me on the airplane [on a flight to England, on the public address system], and the rest is history.*

Towards the end of the 1990s, it was clear that McLachlin was a leading contender to replace Antonio Lamer as chief justice whenever he retired.[85] But there were other senior members of the court who were apparently lobbying for the chief justice position,[86] and so McLachlin's elevation to the chief justiceship was not a foregone conclusion.

4

To the Centre Chair — McLachlin and the Chief Justiceship

On January 7, 2000, Beverley McLachlin became the seventeenth chief justice of the Supreme Court of Canada, elevated from the position of associate justice that she had held for eleven years. In the jargon, she "assumed the centre chair" because it is the centre chair of the row of nine that the chief justice fills when the full court sits in the Supreme Court chamber. At the time she was appointed, she became the first woman chief justice in the history of the Court and the third youngest person to become chief justice;[1] by the time she retired on December 15, 2017, she had become the longest serving chief justice in the history of the institution.[2] These facts should be placed in a broader institutional and historical context to clarify what it means for a member of the court to become chief justice, and what it means to the court to have a new chief justice.

Formally, the chief justice is appointed in the same way as all the other members of the court — by the governor general, acting on the advice of the prime minister. The office of chief justice is and always has been identified within the *Supreme Court Act* itself —

section 4(1) says that the Court shall consist of a chief justice and eight[3] "puisne"[4] judges, and section 4(2) says they are appointed by the Governor in Council "in letters patent under the Great Seal." Notice that it does not say, "The Supreme Court shall consist of nine judges, one of whom shall be designated as chief justice" — this would result in a very different relationship between the chief justice and the associate justices.[5] Instead, the chief justiceship is singled out as a distinctly separate appointment with its own guarantee of tenure; Canada's Supreme Court chief justices never "return to the ranks."

In Canada, the practice is for that appointment to be made from among the current members of the Court, there having been only a single "parachute" appointment from outside the Court directly into the centre chair in the history of the institution: Charles Fitzpatrick in 1906.[6] This situation makes an interesting contrast with the Supreme Court of the United States, whose chief justice is almost always appointed from outside the Court. The fact that there has been only a single exception in Canada in almost 150 years makes the point: when there is a vacancy for the Canadian chief justiceship, the eight candidates are the other judges already serving on the Court.

During the 1990s, a credible candidate for the chief justiceship to succeed Lamer was Frank Iacobucci. He had been a solid member of the group of judges that had clearly centred the Court through the Lamer decade. When the Lamer Court divided, which it did rather frequently, Iacobucci was usually on the winning side, and more often than not the rest of the winning side included Lamer, Cory, Sopinka and Major. Iacobucci was clearly one of the leading members of the "gang of five." He had a very long string of major decisions to his credit — decisions that dealt with controversial issues (signalling immediate importance) and were frequently cited by the court in its later cases (speaking to persisting importance). He had the further distinction, along with his colleague Peter Cory, of having more or less invented the Court's modern style of co-authored judgments, an important development. In comparison, McLachlin had been something of an outlier, frequently differing from the majority position and writing many dissents and separate concurrences, often alone. In much of the decade's academic commentary on the court, she tended not to wear the maverick label for the simple reason that her colleague Claire L'Heureux-Dubé differed even more frequently, more colourfully and at greater length. If the Supreme Court could be thought of as having an "establishment" in 2000, Iacobucci would have been considered the "establishment" candidate for the chief justiceship, and McLachlin the long-shot outsider.

However, the selection of a Canadian Supreme Court chief justice depends on two traditions that very much constrain the prime minister's choice. The first and most venerable tradition is seniority. For the entire history of the Supreme Court, the best predictor of the next chief justice was simply "the most senior of the associate justices." This is not only an after-the-fact observation, but an operating expectation of the legal profession and the wider public, not infrequently mentioned by the prime minister of the day in announcing the appointment.

On the very rare occasions when it was violated — most famously, when the very junior Bora Laskin was named chief justice over the very senior Ronald Martland in 1973 — this was not only surprising but also controversial and even objectionable to some. The Canadian Bar Association formally complained to Prime Minister Pierre Trudeau about the departure from tradition, claiming that it compromised the court's judicial independence for a chief justice to be appointed on the basis of a discretionary choice by the prime minister. Given the then-controversial positions advanced by Professor Laskin (as he was before he became Justice Laskin) on such matters as entrenched human rights and the federal/provincial balance of powers emerging from the Canadian Constitution, this was more than an abstract or hypothetical issue.

One consequence of Canada's seniority tradition, combined

(since 1927) with mandatory retirement at seventy-five, is that Canadian chief justices usually have shorter periods of service than their American counterparts.[7] McLachlin was the seventeenth chief justice of the Supreme Court of Canada. As it happened, her American counterpart for the early years of her chief justiceship, Chief Justice William Rehnquist, was also the seventeenth chief justice of that Supreme Court, even though the U.S. Court has existed for almost ninety years longer than the Canadian Supreme Court. The typical Canadian chief justice has served for about a dozen years as an associate justice before becoming chief; the typical U.S. chief justice is appointed from outside the court, never serving as an associate justice at all. The average length of service of a chief justice in the United States — where there is no mandatory retirement age for judges — is thirteen years; the average length of service for a Canadian chief justice is eight years. McLachlin's eighteen years made her by far the longest serving chief justice in Canadian history, but it would only have placed her fifth among the U.S. chief justices.[8]

The slight qualifier to the "most senior" rule that seems to have been in play in more recent decades is an age factor. The record shows that seniority does not apply if it would result in the appointment as chief justice of a judge who is seventy-two or older. This is an accommodation to the statutory requirement for chief justices to retire at the age of seventy-five. Building on the Canadian practice of appointing from within the court, appointing a chief somewhat over seventy would lead to a very short chief justiceship, and a series of these could be problematic.[9] Absent this implicit codicil, the "most senior" rule would have given the chief justiceship to Claire L'Heureux-Dubé, who reached retirement age in 2002.

The second tradition that has been in play more recently is that of an alternation between francophone and anglophone (that is to say, Quebec and non-Quebec) chief justices, reflecting the bijural nature of the Canadian judicial system. Remarkably, these two traditions have almost never collided. For decades, "most senior" complemented rather than conflicted with "French/English alternation." The only exception was the choice of Brian Dickson to replace Bora Laskin in 1984; the alternation principle would have pointed to the slightly more junior Jean Beetz. When McLachlin stepped down in 2017, there was again a conflict between the principles, with seniority pointing to Andromache Karakatsanis and alternation to Richard Wagner, with the choice going to Wagner. In 2000, however, alternation was not an issue: both Iacobucci and McLachlin would have satisfied it.

The point is that when we say "the prime minister chooses," that really means at most choosing between two competing traditions, and more often simply "choosing" the one person who satisfies both of them. At first glance this might seem a strange way to handle such an important decision. It would seem more reasonable to allow the prime minister to choose the most distinguished, or the most intellectually respected, or the most managerially competent of the alternatives, which may or may not also point us to the most senior judge. However, the traditions reinforce the independence of the judiciary from the political executive, in a way that a less constrained choice by a partisan political official would not.[10]

It is almost always the case that the prime minister who names someone to the chief justiceship is not the same person, and often not even from the same political party, as the prime minister who made that person's initial appointment to the court. McLachlin was appointed to the Supreme Court by Progressive Conservative Prime Minister Brian Mulroney, and then elevated to the chief justiceship by Liberal Prime Minister Jean Chrétien. Wagner in turn was appointed by Conservative Prime Minister Stephen Harper and then elevated to the chief justiceship by Liberal Prime Minister Justin Trudeau. This makes it much harder to stick a partisan tag on a chief justice in the way that comparable judges are routinely identified in the United States.

McLachlin completely satisfied both forks of the "prime minister does not really have a choice" criteria that have for many years directed the choice of a new chief justice. To have picked anyone other than McLachlin (even a judge as experienced and respected as Iacobucci) would have been the profoundly controversial choice.

WHAT CHIEF JUSTICES DO

After McLachlin moved from associate justice to chief justice, she became the "first among equals." As it happens, this is also the standard (and perhaps somewhat dated) description of the position of the prime minister within the cabinet, but the apparent parallel is highly misleading. Unlike the prime minister, the chief justice does not appoint her own colleagues, does not deploy the positive and negative incentives of promotion and demotion among differently ranked posts and certainly lacks the ultimate weapon of removing colleagues who are underperforming or uncooperative. This being the case, a chief justice is considerably less "first" and much more "equal" than a prime minister.

The "equal" part is obvious. Hers is one voice around the post-hearing conference table and one "vote" as to the outcome; she is one of the nine judges who take not-necessarily-equal turns at writing the judgments. This equal status is enhanced by the protocol in the post-hearing judicial conferences. The Canadian chief justice is the last to speak to indicate an opinion on the case; in the United States, the chief justice speaks first. Chief justices do not even have any differentiating insignia on the court's formal ermine robes in Canada, while U.S. Chief Justice Rehnquist added gold stripes on the sleeves of his judicial gown. Canadian chief justices are not likely to entertain such ideas. At the same time, however, Canadian chief justices in this modern era unquestionably have a higher profile and greater visibility than their associate justice colleagues, and it would be carrying matters too far to suggest that there is no difference at all. Chief justices might be "equal" in many senses, but they are also "first" in ways that cannot be overlooked.

The first component of the chief justice's duties might be

described as "business as usual." Chief justices continue to do the same thing as all the other judges on the court, the same things they did before they became chief justice. They sit on panels, read the submissions of litigants and interveners, hear oral arguments and interact with their colleagues to generate decisions (outcomes, in the form of "appeal allowed" or "appeal dismissed") that are supported by extended explanatory reasons. Should they not agree with the majority, they can write (or sign on to a colleague's) minority reasons, in the form of dissents (disagreeing with the outcome) or separate concurrences (disagreeing with the reasons supporting that outcome). Some chief justices, like Lamer, were willing to write minority reasons as often as most of their colleagues. Others, like McLachlin, were much more self-constrained in this respect.

Unlike its American counterpart, the Supreme Court of Canada does not always sit with the full panel of nine judges. Instead, it has used a range of panel sizes. As noted earlier, five, seven and nine are the obvious choices, with even numbers being avoided because of the possible awkwardness of even division.[11] Generally speaking, as one would expect, the panel size reflects the case to be heard — larger panels are used for major cases, smaller panels for more routine ones. Because the chief justiceship involves many other duties, some chief justices have tended to sit on fewer panels than their colleagues (tilted, of course, towards the more important cases). However, in this respect McLachlin was very much an exception. For most of her eighteen years in this role, the simple count of her panel appearances has put her at the top of the list, including a good number of the five-judge panels that deal with more routine matters.

Since McLachlin became chief justice, there has been a gradually declining number of decisions handed down each year. This does not mean that the Court has not been working as hard as before. A good part of the decline is accounted for by a 1999 amendment to the *Supreme Court Act* that reduced the number of appeals by right (that is to say, reviews of decisions by provincial courts of appeal that the Supreme Court must hear regardless of whether or not they raise any major question of law). Most of these had been dealt with very routinely — often in a short single sentence decision dismissing the appeal "for the reasons given in the court below," yet they counted towards the total annual number of cases decided by the Court. In addition, the reduced number of cases has been offset by a steady growth in the average size of the Supreme Court panels that consider them, so that the workload of the average judge has changed much less than the decisions-per-year number would seem to suggest.[12]

The second part of the chief justice's job might be described as "business as usual plus" — additional responsibilities on both sides of the hearing and decision process described above. Administrative matters such as deciding the size of the panel for specific cases, and which judges sit on which of the smaller panels fall to the chief justice. No reader will fail to notice that there is an opportunity here to steer the process by including certain judges and excluding others. Andrew Heard suggested, based on statistical analysis, that some such selectivity had been involved in *Charter* cases in the 1990s.[13] This issue has become increasingly moot as a result of a relentless shift towards larger panels. Five-judge panels (which before the 1960s accounted for most of the decisions) are now reserved for Quebec civil law appeals, and for minor cases, mostly appeals by right that raise no large issues and can be dealt with briefly and orally, whose number has been sharply reduced by the 1999 amendments. Conversely, nine-judge panels have become much more frequent, and the intermediate seven-judge panels have become more unusual. The seven-judge panels in the McLachlin Court often resulted from one or more of the judges not being available.[14]

More significantly, the chief justice plays a major role in the decision-making process after the oral argument. The practice since the early 1960s has been for the panel members to meet in conference immediately after the hearing to discuss their view on the case and its issues, a process which goes around the room from most junior to most senior so that everyone is expected to contribute. If a consensus emerges as to the outcome and the focus of the supporting reasons, a decision is made as to which of the justices should undertake the writing of the judgment (subject to the circulation of the draft for critical comments by the others).[15]

From the way judges describe this process in interviews,[16] volunteering is a major component of the process, with seniority as a significant "tie-breaker," although the chief justice may sometimes ask — or, more rarely and unusually, actually direct — that a particular individual do the writing. During the McLachlin chief justiceship, the writing of the decision has increasingly often been undertaken not by a single justice (long the traditional way for common law courts to operate) but jointly by two or three or even more of the judges. The assignment usually happens at the conference itself, but on occasion it will take several days before it is made.

As well, the chief justice is formally responsible for the organization and administration of the Supreme Court, which in 2017 was a $33 million operation, with a full-time staff of more than two hundred.[17] In practice, the day-to-day responsibility for overseeing this aspect of the Supreme Court's operations is assigned to the registrar of the Supreme Court, who is comparable to a deputy minister. The registrar is accountable to the chief justice.

The chief justice is also involved in a number of ex officio obligations — membership on other bodies by virtue of being chief justice. The most important of these is chairing the Canadian Judicial Council. Established in 1971, this body includes the chief justices, associate chief justices and some additional senior judges from provincial and federal superior courts across the country, for a total membership in 2019 of thirty-nine. The council is responsible for dealing with complaints about the conduct of Canada's 1,300 federally appointed judges; such complaints are investigated by committees of inquiry that report to the council. A possible outcome of this process is a recommendation by the council that the judge in question be removed from office.[18]

This is something more than a remote and unlikely contingency. During the years when McLachlin was chief justice, and therefore president of the Canadian Judicial Council, the council recommended removal of two sitting judges.[19] The council is also involved in organizing seminars for federally appointed judges and coordinating discussions about issues of concern to the Canadian judiciary.

The chief justice chairs the Advisory Council for the Order of Canada, although this role does not give her a vote on individual candidates for the award except on the very rare occasion of a tied vote. The board's votes are almost always unanimous. A rare example of division (although not to the extent of a tie[20]), and one of the Order's most controversial appointments, was that of abortion advocate Henry Morgentaler in 2008. The chief justice also abstains from voting (even in case of a tie) on decisions involving the removal of an individual from the Order, something that happened five times during McLachlin's tenure.

Under the *Letters of Patent of 1947*, the chief justice becomes the administrator of Canada (exercising all the powers and duties of the governor general) should the governor general die, become incapacitated or be absent from the country for a period of more than one month. This has only happened three times in Canada's history, the third being in 2005 when McLachlin was so designated while Governor General Adrienne Clarkson was hospitalized to have a pacemaker installed.

Another area of the chief justice's responsibility involves being the face and "voice of the court," speaking for the institution in a way that none of her colleagues are comparably positioned to do, which is not to deny that all the members of the court play a much more public role than was the case a few decades ago. It is worth remembering as well that the chief justice is the voice not only of the Supreme Court itself, but also of the Canadian judiciary in a broader sense. According to the *Supreme Court Act*, her title is not "Chief Justice of the Supreme Court of Canada," but rather "Chief Justice of Canada." It is in this capacity that the chief justice spoke out on issues such as trial court delays or the problematically slow pace of judicial appointments to the lower courts.

This "public face" aspect has become an important component of the role. Fifty years ago, we would hardly have mentioned it, because the Supreme Court and the judiciary in general had a very low public profile. There is no record that Chief Justice Patrick Kerwin in the 1950s, or Chief Justice J.R. Cartwright in the 1960s, ever did a sit-down interview with a journalist. But this began to change in the 1970s in a number of ways that we generally associate with the Laskin court (1973–1984), coinciding with a steady increase in the number of constitutional cases in the Supreme Court caseload.

The *Charter of Rights*, after its 1982 entrenchment in the Canadian Constitution, ratcheted up the court's visibility considerably as the impact of the *Charter* rippled through Canadian government and society. The Court has felt this impact in two areas: first, it is faced with a larger number of highly controversial issues, and second, it is expected to explain itself in a wider variety of ways to a more broadly conceived audience. Today, no discussion of any new or proposed public policy could take place without contemplating what the reaction of the court might be. One of the major developments of Canadian political life over the last half century has been the emergence of the Supreme Court as a major element of Canadian governance broadly considered, and the dramatic expansion of its role as a constitutional court. Fifty years ago, the court rarely dealt with more than one constitutional case a year, but now such cases usually make up a quarter of the caseload.

This "voice of the court" role is called for in three rather different sets of circumstances. The first is formal liaison between the court and the federal government, which in practice generally means the minister of justice but can on occasion mean the prime minister. This raises the paradox at the core of the concept of judicial independence. On one hand, the courts must operate at arm's length from government, insulated from direct pressure before, or possible retaliation after, any of its decisions that have a significant impact on government policy or operations. On the other hand, they constantly rely on government for support and services and they may anticipate problems or issues that can be dealt with more smoothly if they are given some careful consideration before they actually materialize. This is a delicate balance in evolving circumstances. Certainly the very close relationship between (for example) Prime Minister Mackenzie King and Chief Justice Lyman Duff in the 1940s[21] would not be acceptable today, nor would any attempt to influence the court's handling (or even timing) of a case. Still, it is an ongoing responsibility of the chief justice that can demand careful attention.

The chief justice–prime minister relationship sometimes can go wrong, and when it does the consequences can be dramatic. In any future analysis of court-government relations, the McLachlin Court will long be remembered for the very public confrontation between the prime minister and the chief justice that occurred in the context of the Nadon affair in 2014, discussed later in the book.

The second aspect of the chief justice's role as voice of the court involves representing the court to the broader Canadian public. This was signalled very dramatically by the circumstances of McLachlin's elevation. Both when she was named as "chief justice-elect" in the summer of 1999, and then again when she assumed the position in early 2000, she "did the rounds" of the national media, doing sit-down interviews with television and radio and newspapers and news magazines alike. McLachlin credits Lamer with having pointed out this public obligation to her. McLachlin's performances during these interviews was masterful. Her wording was precise, revealing careful thought and advance preparation, and she managed to maintain a disarming freshness through the repetitions of the many interviews. A more formal aspect of this same responsibility is the chief justice's interaction with the bar and academia, illustrated by the constant string of speeches, papers and other presentations.[22]

The third aspect of the chief justice's role as voice of the Court is international. This too is a recent development. Even a few decades ago, judges rarely interacted with their colleagues across provincial boundaries, let alone national ones. Now judges (and especially chief justices) interact frequently with their global colleagues in a variety of venues, not to mention the constant exchanges that routinely take place on chat-boards of secure websites. This interaction is very much enhanced by the way that judicial decisions for many countries are available online more or less as soon as they are handed down in the courtroom. Whatever a term like "the globalization of judicial power" might eventually come to mean, today it includes at the very least these constant meetings and exchanges. When Lady Brenda Hale, the president of the United Kingdom Supreme Court, spoke at an academic conference reflecting on McLachlin's career, her comments were replete with casual "Beverley and I" references.[23] As one manifestation of the international dimensions of modern appellate judicial performance, within weeks of leaving the court McLachlin announced that she had accepted appointments on the Singapore International Commercial Court and the Hong Kong Court of Final Appeal.[24]

We asked McLachlin to comment on the difference between being chief justice and associate justice. Here is her answer:

> *Being chief justice involved a lot more responsibilities and a lot more work. You have a number of administrative responsibilities for the whole Court in fact, and keeping the rota, setting the rota, making sure the judgments get out, signing judgments, assigning people to sit on judgments, sometimes assigning writing, making sure that colleagues all get along as much as they can,*

promoting collegiality, going to and planning a lot of court events.

There are a lot of things I haven't mentioned like law staff, budgeting, all those kinds of things. The registrar is there to do a lot of it, and the staff are wonderful, but as chief justice under the [Supreme Court] *Act, as you know, the chief justice is responsible for how the organization runs, so I took that very seriously. I've never been someone who declines to delegate — I believe in delegation. But at the same time, you have to have your finger on all those things, and when decisions have to be made, you have to do that, and it takes a lot of time.*

The other additional duties are the Canadian Judicial Council, which you chair, the National Judicial Institute, which is the [judicial] education branch; you chair the meeting of the Order of Canada; there are meetings and speaking engagements across the country in much greater number. When I was an associate justice, I used to do things more related to what you would call continuing legal education, but as chief justice I did less of that and more representational speaking, where I would talk about the rule of law, the role of the Court, how the Court goes about its job.

Plus, I do a number of lectures, because you get invitations to these lectures, both national and international, and that's the final part. As chief justice you get a lot of international representational work, and I took that very seriously because I felt that I was very proud of the Court and Canadian jurisprudence, and the story we had to tell, with our recent adoption of the Charter, *and many of our cases would be increasingly discussed around the world, and Canada became a place people started look to jurisprudentially. I got a lot of invitations to international conferences, and that took a lot of time too. The*

> *workload was much heavier. And it's heavy enough as*
> *an associate justice — the preparation for cases, writing*
> *judgments and some outside work is already a big job.*
> *What it meant was longer days, longer hours.*[25]

The work described above obviously implies a rather heavy workload. In the 1990s, we asked Chief Justice Lamer about the difference in the workload between an associate judge and the chief justice. We mentioned to McLachlin that Lamer told us that he continued to work 100 per cent as a judge, but there was an additional 40 per cent added on by the additional responsibilities of the chief justice.[26] McLachlin commented, "That's about right. I did that, maybe even higher than 40."[27]

At one time, now decades past, an appointment to an appellate court was widely thought to imply an easing away from the pressures of a lawyer's life — "time to brush up on your golf game."[28] The preceding paragraphs completely belie any such suggestion, especially for the "work load plus" of a chief justice. Reading the files to prepare for pending cases, sitting to hear oral arguments in current cases, writing up the reasons (and commenting on the drafts of others) for reserved cases, supervisory interactions involving a significant administrative structure, preparing talks and speeches and travelling to present them, attending national and international conferences, presiding over statutory committees — this calls for an exceptional work ethic and an unusual energy level. In addition, during her final year on the court, McLachlin somehow made enough time to write a subsequently-published novel. Anyone who believes that today's appellate judges are enjoying something of a semi-retirement from law practice simply is not paying attention.

WHY DO CHIEF JUSTICES MATTER?

The most obvious way for justices to have lasting influence is through the reasons they express in their decisions and the way those reasons are accepted and built upon by the Court in subsequent decisions. To be followed and cited and directly quoted is the major way that justices can have a lasting impact on the law, and thereby on the lives and choices of many people who many not even know which judicial decision nudged the world around them in that direction. Since the chief justice decides who will write majority judgments, she obviously can choose to write the judgments on major cases that are most important to her, a privilege reinforced by the fact that the modern chief justice might well be assumed to "speak for the Court" on at least some of the Court's highest-profile decisions.

The major counter to the chief justice's prerogative to write the Court's leading decisions is the simple fact that the chief justice must be in the majority before she can assign herself to write the judgment. Beyond that, however, if the chief justice is first among equals, the bedrock foundation of that equality is that every judge has an equal vote. The balance between votes to allow or dismiss, or to follow this or that line of argument in explanation, constrains the choice of who will write for the majority. Further, being too heavy-handed or too selfish about the allocation of judgment writing erodes the collegiality that is always important to the Supreme Court and was particularly important to this chief justice. In fact, McLachlin has utterly transformed the process of determining which judge or judges will write a judgment, a very important development in its own right but one that has further constrained the potential that self-assigning judgments might have been thought to provide.

It is also significant that the chief justice chairs the post-hearing conference and guides its deliberations. An adroit and respected chairperson can have a profound influence on the outcome. As noted above, the chief justice is the person who formally decides who will write the judgment for the majority even when she does not take on the duty herself. This decision may involve balancing between several volunteers or making her own suggestion as to who might write, or encouraging co-authorship rather than solo authorship, or patiently discouraging minority reasons even as she curbs her own earlier predilection for solo writing. A little later in the process, the Court has a strict practice of circulating and subsequently revising draft judgments, which gives the chief justice a further opportunity for persuasive intervention.

We suggest that the influence of a Canadian chief justice is enhanced by the fact that the chiefs are practically always appointed from within the court rather than parachuted from outside, which means that they have a measure of direct experience within the institution that normally exceeds that of most if not all of their colleagues around the table. This seniority of experience increases as time goes on and new judges replace the veterans. As long as this "institutional memory" is not overplayed, it can often help to tilt the balance.

This is not so much power as the opportunity for influence. But the opportunity for influence looks a lot like power when it is deployed carefully and effectively, and that would seem to be the appropriate description for McLachlin. Its success should not be taken for granted, as earlier chief justices sometimes learned. Laskin, for example, spent at least the first half of his chief justiceship writing a relatively high number of minority reasons, frustrated by a voting combination of the "Diefenbaker trio" (Ronald Martland, Roland Ritchie, Wilfred Judson) and the Quebec judges that often left him in the minority.[29] Subsequent chief justices have enjoyed better circumstances.

The first measure of a judge's impact is still the judgments written and the persisting impact of those decisions on the handling of subsequent cases. To the extent that chief justices exercise an influence other than the one expressed through their authored judgments, the measure of McLachlin's impact involves the whole range of decisions that were created by the Court under her leadership.

5

The Historical Impact of the McLachlin Court

McLachlin retired from hearing cases on December 14, 2017, and Richard Wagner became chief justice on December 18. However, the *Supreme Court Act* provides that judges continue to be members of the Court for a further six months after retirement to participate in decisions in cases heard by panels that they had been part of prior to retirement, where these panels had reserved judgment. They can still be fully involved in the ongoing deliberations, drafting majority judgments or minority reasons or signing on to the reasons of others. After that six-month period, they cease to be eligible for such participation.[1] McLachlin's formal retirement from the court took place on December 15, 2017, but she participated in her last delivered judgment on June 15, 2018, pushing the six months to its limit.[2] To this extent, the term McLachlin Court actually includes a six-month overlap between the era of the previous chief justice and that of the new one.[3]

A mere fifty years ago the Supreme Court of Canada was described as a "quiet court."[4] For much of its history, it was rare for it to be in the public eye and even rarer for it to be an intrusion on the political life of the nation. Since the entrenchment of the *Charter*, however, the Court has become a significant element in Canadian politics and public life, and the actions and decisions of the McLachlin Court have made it a significant force in the Canadian story for the first two decades of this century. We remember the Laskin Court for the *Patriation Reference*; we remember the Dickson Court for its decisions setting the frame for the then-new *Charter of Rights*; we remember the Lamer Court for its sometimes provocative application of the *Charter* to broader swaths of Canadian law and practice. The McLachlin Court will be remembered both for some of its decisions discussed below and for the increased level of collegiality it applied in reaching and formalizing those decisions.

Let us begin with its constitutional decisions. At one time, the Court handed down about one constitutional decision per year and in many years delivered none, but those days are long past. A complete list of the McLachlin Court's constitutional decisions would stretch into the hundreds. Narrowing the list to a reasonable length and then organizing it thematically therefore presents a challenge. Nevertheless, constitutional issues can be broadly sorted into three areas: the *Charter*, Indigenous issues and federalism.

THE McLACHLIN COURT'S *CHARTER* DECISIONS

Section 7: Life, Liberty and Security of the Person

Section 7 of the *Charter* provides that everyone has a right to "life, liberty and security of the person," and this has become one of the more important elements of the *Charter*. It is treated not as three different rights but as three different "interests" of a single right, with the major emphasis falling on "security of the person."

One of the McLachlin Court's highest-profile cases involved section 7's entrenchment of the "right to life": the 2015 *Carter* decision on assisted suicide.[5] Twenty years earlier, in a divided decision in

1993, the court had upheld the *Criminal Code* provisions prohibiting assisted suicide, ruling that assisted suicide was not consistent
with the value placed on human life by the *Charter*'s section 7
guarantee.[6] Revisiting the question in 2015, the Court unanimously
decided that the absolute prohibition of assisted suicide was not
consistent with the *Charter* and struck down the relevant portions
of the *Criminal Code*. Upon rendering this decision, the Court
suspended the effect of its declaration of invalidity to allow the
government time to correct the legislation — an approach that has
become the Court's preferred remedial response.[7]

Equally intriguing was the remedial follow-up to *Carter*, in the
case we might call "*Carter 2*."[8] Rather than proceeding with the
legislative process to amend the *Criminal Code* in response to the
Court's ruling, the Harper government instead focused on the 2015
election campaign, which it ultimately lost. When the new Liberal
government took office, the time limit for the suspended declaration of invalidity had almost elapsed, so the new government
applied for an extension.

That extension naturally involved the continuing application
of the admittedly invalid law to those individuals who wished to
exercise the infringed right, and although the Court unanimously
granted the extension, it split 5–4 on this remedy issue. The majority used the concept of a "constitutional exemption" to create a
procedure that would address the small set of individuals during
the continued suspension of invalidity. *Charter* remedies (the
Court's statement of what will happen when it finds that government action has infringed a *Charter* right unjustifiably) raise
complex issues in their own right, and this notion of a "constitutional exemption" is something that the Court has tentatively
explored — but generally backed away from — a number of times
since the 1990s. "*Carter 2*" therefore somewhat revived a remedial
option that most commentators (and some earlier Court decisions)
had declared effectively dead.

Two of the McLachlin Court's decisions have contributed to

an understanding of the right to security of the person, also guaranteed under section 7 of the *Charter: Insite*[9] and *Bedford*.[10] Both cases were decided unanimously, and both decisions were written by McLachlin.

The Insite case[11] concerned the Harper government's decision to shut down the safe injection site that had been established in Vancouver as part of a response to the public health emergency posed by rampant addiction in the city's Downtown Eastside. Since the drugs in question were illegal, this program required an exemption from the normal impact of the federal criminal law, and the government's refusal to renew that exemption generated the case. Supporters of *Insite* argued that the federal government lacked the necessary legislative jurisdiction, but this argument was brushed aside by the Supreme Court, which found that the critical question involved the policy's impact on the right to life and security of the person. Where a supervised injection site would decrease the risk of death and disease and where there was no evidence of a negative impact on public safety, it ruled that the federal minister of health could not refuse to grant the exemption.[12]

The *Bedford* case[13] involved a section 7 *Charter* challenge to the federal criminal law provisions on prostitution. The plaintiffs argued that since prostitution itself is not illegal, certain aspects of the criminal law that prevent prostitutes from implementing safety measures (such as hiring security guards or screening potential clients) restrict security of the person to such an extent that they are unconstitutional.

Somewhat unusually, the matter had been considered by the Court before, in the 1990 *Prostitution Reference*,[14] and the challenged aspects of the criminal law had at that time been upheld as constitutionally valid. During the trial stage of *Bedford*, the judge distinguished the 1990 decision, noting that the extensive evidence presented to the trial court about the harm caused by the criminal law in question had not been available to the judges in 1990. It was unusual for a trial judge to put aside a Supreme Court precedent and to rule the other way, and unusual again for the Supreme Court itself not to condemn such temerity, but instead to accept and even commend it. A unanimous Supreme Court ruled that the challenged sections of the *Criminal Code* violated the section 7 rights of prostitutes by preventing them from taking reasonable measures to promote their own safety and that the measures could not be justified as reasonable limits on those rights. The Court invoked what has become its standard remedy, a declaration of invalidity which was suspended for one year to allow Parliament to come up with appropriate new legislation.

Freedom of Association and Labour Rights

Perhaps less dramatically, but certainly with much wider practical repercussions, the McLachlin Court also revisited the Supreme Court's earlier decisions on freedom of association and its implications for collective bargaining and labour unions. Those earlier decisions, starting with the 1987 *Labour Trilogy*,[15] had flatly rejected suggestions that "freedom of association" in section 2 of the *Charter* effectively entrenched collective bargaining, with its possible concomitant implications of a right to strike. (Note: The 1987 decision was released two years before McLachlin joined the Supreme Court.)

The majority decision interpreted freedom of association narrowly as simply an individual's ability to do in association with others, activities that they otherwise had the right to engage in as individuals. The minority reasons, written by Chief Justice Dickson and concurred in by Justice Bertha Wilson, maintained that unless freedom of association included the right to bargain collectively and to strike under some circumstances, freedom of association had little meaning for unions. Repeated attempts by the unions to challenge the majority determinations were rebuffed by a divided Court for many years.

Worse yet from the point of view of the unions, another case (*Lavigne*[16]) came very close to ruling that the "Rand System," which had prevailed in Canadian labour relations for decades, was itself a constitutional violation, saved only as a "reasonable limit" under section 1 of the *Charter*. Contrary to some expectations in the early 1980s, when federal NDP leader Ed Broadbent had been a strong supporter of entrenching the *Charter*, for its first two decades it was not at all a "union-friendly" document.

The unions were much more successful during the McLachlin era. The first indication came very early, with *Dunmore*.[17] The factual background is complicated: labour laws in all provinces have excluded agricultural workers from the legislation providing for organization and collective bargaining. In Ontario an NDP government had amended the legislation to end this exclusion, and a new Conservative government was attempting to repeal that amendment to once again exclude agricultural workers. Unsurprisingly, the workers challenged this in court. More surprisingly — given the unions' track record in the Supreme Court thus far — they won.

The main decision was written by Michel Bastarache, with McLachlin and six other judges concurring.[18] Bastarache argued that the majority decision in the Alberta labour reference did not explicitly reject a right to collective bargaining and that the majority in 1987 had not explicitly rejected some arguments by Dickson and Wilson in favour of the idea that freedom of association protected collective bargaining rights. The court declared in *Dunmore* that Ontario's blanket prohibition of farm workers' unions was unconstitutional, without having to overrule the decision in the *Alberta Labour Reference*. Furthermore, in ruling that the attempted exclusion of agricultural workers was unconstitutional, the judges made strong positive comments about workers' rights and the importance of workers' associations.

There was more: a few years later, in *B.C. Health Services*,[19] the court repudiated the new B.C. government's attempts to unilaterally roll back contractual agreements with a broad swath of provincial employees' organizations. The six-judge majority decision, jointly written by Beverley McLachlin and Louis LeBel, explicitly overruled the *Labour Trilogy* decision.[20] Even more unusually, the reasons of McLachlin and LeBel in the *B.C. Health Services* decision explicitly adopted the dissenting reasons of Dickson and Wilson in the *Labour Trilogy* and directly rejected the majority reasoning of that earlier judgment.

The 1987 decision, they argued, had been made without sufficient grounding in the context of Canadian labour relations, including Canada's longstanding support for the International Labour Organization's Convention Concerning Freedom of Association and Protection of the Right to Organize.[21] As well, they said, it is important to interpret section 2(d) consistently with other *Charter* rights such as the right to equality.

McLachlin and LeBel pointed out that *Charter* rights are underpinned by broader democratic values that underlie the *Charter*, such as "human dignity, equality, liberty, respect for the autonomy of the person and the enhancement of democracy."[22] Collective bargaining contributes to these underlying values.[23] They found that the *Charter* right to freedom of association included the right of workers to organize for the purposes of collective bargaining, and that this in turn created an employer's duty to negotiate in good faith. However, they declined to address the question of whether this extended to a "right to strike." A divided and somewhat confused decision in *Fraser*[24] in 2011 suggested something of a retreat, but the Court took the next major step on the subject in 2015 with *Saskatchewan Federation of Labour*,[25] holding in a majority decision written by Rosalie Abella that the *Charter* right to freedom of association did indeed include the right to strike.

The decision remains controversial, if only for implicitly retreating from earlier firm statements by the Supreme Court that the *Charter* did not entrench any economic rights. We see from this decision, however, that under the McLachlin Court the *Charter* has come to have a major impact on Canadian labour law as legislative amendments ripple across the country. While it may seem that the

Court was simply confirming what had long been common practice, there are in fact a number of occupations that had been quite routinely denied the right to strike, such as agricultural workers, workers in essential services (fire, emergency, police) and, rather more curiously, academic staff at Alberta universities. On the other hand, these decisions do not mean that governments cannot still place restrictions on the right to strike, just that in doing so they must now satisfy the "*Oakes* test" for reasonable limits under section 1 of the *Charter*.[26]

Freedom of Religion

Given that the Canadian *Charter of Rights and Freedoms* has been an entrenched part of the Canadian Constitution since 1982, and that one of those entrenched elements was "freedom of religion," it is surprising how long it took for the Court to deal with the very basic question of what "religion" actually means in this context. An early *Charter* decision (*Big M Drug Mart*)[27] identified what the "freedom" half of this phrase meant — it included freedom of belief, freedom to declare those beliefs openly and freedom to manifest those beliefs through both acts of worship and proselytization — but did not directly address the "religion" half. Such reticence is understandable, given the changing public status of religion over time.

The McLachlin Court grasped this nettle firmly in 2004, in *Amselem*.[28] The precipitating issue involved the construction of a temporary structure (a "succah") on a condo balcony despite the fact that condo regulations clearly prohibited it, with the action being defended as a religious practice. A divided decision dramatically presented the two obvious poles for the definition of religion on which the case hinged.

The dissent would have upheld the prohibition by anchoring the concept of religion to the established and shared beliefs and practices of an established religious community — thus using orthodoxy as the central defining notion. But the majority stated that religion was to be understood in more individualized terms as personal adherence to a set of ideas connected to the divine or eternal — thus establishing sincerity as the central defining notion. The decision shifted the emphasis for freedom of religion away from history and larger organizations towards smaller and newer (even completely individual) understandings of religion.

Although it was a divided decision by the smallest possible majority, the decision has not been significantly revisited.[29] More recent cases have dealt with the scope of the right in the face of various forms of regulation — how big a hurdle must governments overcome when invoking a "reasonable limit" under section 1 of the *Charter*.

In *Multani*,[30] the Court vigorously upheld freedom of religion by defending the right of Sikh children to wear a small kirpan[31] sewn securely into their clothing at school. In *Hutterian Brethren*,[32] however, the Court ruled that members of a religious community that objected to photographs on their driver's licences were not exempt from that regulation because the burden placed on that community could be easily accommodated. In *R. v. N.S.*,[33] the Court left it to the discretion of trial judges whether a witness would be required to remove a face covering during testimony, given the nature of the case and the right of an accused to a fair hearing.

One may say therefore that during the McLachlin chief justiceship the Supreme Court clarified the *Charter* right to freedom of religion, both by providing a more precise definition that would contribute to predictable outcomes and by offering a clearer sense of the robustness with which its invocation will prevail in the face of governmental claims of "reasonable limits."

The fly in the freedom-of-religion ointment came in the *Trinity Western* cases (technically Wagner Court decisions because they were decided after he became chief justice, but heard when McLachlin was still active on the panel as oral argument had preceded her retirement date). Trinity Western is an evangelical Christian postsecondary institution in British Columbia that required students and faculty to adhere to a religiously based code of conduct that, among other things, prohibits "sexual intimacy" outside heterosexual marriage.

An early visit to the Supreme Court involved Trinity Western's application to establish a teachers' college, which the B.C. College of Teachers refused to approve because of the school's "discriminatory practices."[34] On that occasion Trinity Western prevailed, but in 2017 the university was back in front of the court, this time because its proposed law school had been denied approval by the law societies of both British Columbia and Ontario.[35] This time, the university was less successful. Its argument that the student and faculty "Covenant" is protected by the *Charter*'s freedom of religion guarantee was accepted, but the decisions of the two law societies were accepted as a justifiable "reasonable limit" on that freedom. Trinity Western subsequently made the Convenant optional rather than obligatory.

Charter Remedies

Another somewhat unclear legacy of the McLachlin Court involves its handling of *Charter* remedies. If the Court finds that a government has violated a *Charter* right or has limited such a right in a way that does not qualify as a "reasonable limit" under section 1, it then needs to state the remedy for the *Charter* violation. One possibility is strongly implied by section 52 of the *Constitution Act, 1982*: "The Constitution of Canada is the supreme law of Canada, and any law that is inconsistent with the provisions of the Constitution is, to the extent of the inconsistency, of no force and effect." From this perspective, if the Court finds that a statute or a part of a statute is unconstitutional, the result would be as if the offending legislation is simply erased from the statute books.[36] This was the approach the Dickson Court took in the early days of the *Charter*.

However, as *Charter* decisions accumulated, experience suggested that this was an unworkably blunt tool and also that immediate and total invalidation could itself create a legal void with awkward uncertainties. The open-ended wording of the *Charter* itself encourages more imaginative options, with section 24(1) mandating whatever "appropriate and just" remedies the courts might deem appropriate "under the circumstances."

The Court began to consider a spectrum of further responses, with the Lamer Court's decision in *Schachter* providing the most focused early discussion.[37] In this case, the Court found that parental leave benefits in the *Unemployment Insurance Act* at the time discriminated against men. Simply declaring the offending section unconstitutional would have meant increased expenditures for the federal government, something that the Court did not want to cause.

Of lasting significance, the Court in *Schachter* came up with what has become the court's *Charter* remedy of choice: the suspended declaration of invalidity. This involves declaring a statute (or part of a statute) unconstitutional, but then suspending that declaration for a specified length of time (typically, six months or a year) to give the relevant legislature time to devise an appropriate replacement. This has the advantage of preventing the confusion of a legal void. It has the disadvantage of leaving in place a law that has been declared to be an unconstitutional violation of rights. It left the *Charter* as a shield protecting human rights with a judicially mandated hole in it.

The McLachlin Court has expanded the "*Charter* remedy" conversation by exploring some further ideas. One of the earliest examples involved its endorsement of a trial court decision that dealt with a *Charter* violation related to minority language education in Nova Scotia by ordering that government officials periodically report to the judge on their progress towards resolving the minority language complaint. Remedies of this sort were not uncommon in the United States,[38] but they were quite outside the Canadian experience. It was therefore something of a surprise when the Supreme Court upheld the decision on appeal.[39]

A few years later, when a man was mistakenly identified as a potential "pie-thrower" during a prime ministerial visit to Vancouver[40] and was arrested and subjected to a strip search, a trial judge awarded (somewhat nominal) damages for the police department's violation of his *Charter* rights. Again, the Supreme Court upheld this innovation on appeal, with McLachlin writing the judgment for a unanimous Court.[41]

Even more transformative was the notion of remedies that would convert the *Charter* from a negative document — one prohibiting government action that would infringe upon the listed rights — into a positive document — one creating a constitutional obligation for government to undertake certain actions to promote or create the conditions to support those listed rights. If the *Charter* is generally thought of as a shield protecting individual rights from governmental infringement, this would turn it into a sword that would compel positive government action.

The case in which this idea was aired most directly was *Gosselin*, which involved a challenge against programs that reduced benefits to welfare recipients below a certain age unless they were taking part in a public retraining program. Louise Gosselin challenged the program not only for an alleged violation of equality rights (the age limitation), but even more basically on the grounds that her section 7 rights to security of the person were violated by the significant reduction of welfare benefits.[42] The challenge narrowly failed, and McLachlin's reasons for dismissing the claim drew four separate sets of solo dissenting reasons. Louise Arbour's vigorous argument that the *Charter* had created a "positive obligation" upon the state to provide basic protection was striking. McLachlin's decision left that possibility open, but for her this was the wrong case at the wrong time.

Another possible *Charter* remedy involves a "constitutional exemption." This idea takes a number of different forms. Sometimes the courts might uphold a challenged law while identifying and exempting a very small specific set of individuals whose rights would be negatively affected by the law in question. Sometimes, when the remedy of suspended invalidation is employed, the immediate challenging parties in the case are exempted from its application during this hiatus — what the American literature sometimes refers to as a "golden ticket," good for one trip only. Most recently, it was invoked in the "*Carter 2*" decision, allowing a certain set of individuals during the suspended invalidation of the law against assisted suicide to apply to a provincial superior court for a declaration that a doctor who assisted them would not be subject to criminal charges.[43] But the notion of constitutional exemption has never been firmly embraced by the court as a viable option.[44]

A suspended declaration of invalidity (with a possibility of extending the suspension) is still the "remedy of choice" thirty-five years after the entrenchment of the *Charter*. For all its willingness to consider further options that would follow up on the open-ended invitation of "appropriate and just" remedies contained in section 24, the McLachlin Court did not make much progress in this area beyond the Lamer Court that preceded it.[45]

INDIGENOUS ISSUES

The *Charter* has for obvious reasons very much occupied centre stage in the ongoing drama of the Supreme Court's constitutional jurisprudence, but the spotlight may now be swinging to another major constitutional change, namely Aboriginal rights (with its concomitant issues of Aboriginal title and Aboriginal self-government). McLachlin herself acknowledged this, suggesting in a 2014 interview that the issue that would define the Supreme Court in coming years was no longer the *Charter of Rights and Freedoms* but rather the question of reconciliation with First Nations.[46] Again, in an interview on the day of her retirement, it was her Court's contributions to the development of the laws regarding the rights of Indigenous people in which she took particular pride.[47] In a 2015 speech, McLachlin controversially described the residential school system as "attempted cultural genocide" and a "glaring blemish on the Canadian historic record"[48] — not that this was an original idea, but it was surprising to see it publicly endorsed by the chief justice of the highest court in the land.

To some extent, the McLachlin Court's advancement of Aboriginal rights is also the product of the 1982 constitutional changes, with section 35 of the *Constitution Act, 1982* "recognizing and affirming" existing Aboriginal and treaty rights for Aboriginal peoples in Canada. Some of the jurisprudential underpinnings had already been dealt with by earlier decisions: *Guerin's* notion of a governmental "fiduciary responsibility,"[49] *Sparrow's* first serious judicial consideration of section 35 itself,[50] the *Van der Peet Trilogy's* focus on the definition and grounding of Aboriginal rights,[51] and *Delgamuukw's* acceptance of oral history as a valid part of the evidentiary record.[52] The 1999 *Marshall* decisions (with McLachlin dissenting on the initial decision that provoked the controversy[53] and involved in writing the reasons in the "*Marshall 2*" clarification and partial retreat)[54] dramatically demonstrated the potential explosiveness of the issues involved.

In 2004, *Haida Nation* became one of the major decisions of the McLachlin Court.[55] The central concept in this decision involved "the honour of the Crown," which has become a recurrent element of subsequent case law. Put simply, the honour of the Crown obliges the government to "behave honourably" in its dealings with Indigenous peoples and not to "ride rough-shod" over their interests. It is conceptually linked to the notion of fiduciary duty emphasized in the earlier *Guerin* decision, but that notion had been linked to the surrender of Aboriginal land to the control of the Crown, which created an obligation for the government to use that land in a way that serves the best interests of those who surrendered it. The "honour of the Crown" has a much wider reach, because it includes dealings outside as well as within a treaty relationship, which makes it directly relevant to the process of resolving Aboriginal land claims beyond or before a treaty.[56]

The most practical face of "the honour of the Crown" is "the duty to consult" (more completely, "the duty to consult and accommodate").[57] Cases dealing with the details of this implication continue to work their way up the court system. Early examples included RTA[58] and Beckman.[59] Toward the end of McLachlin's chief justiceship, a pair of decisions — Clyde River[60] and Chippewas of the Thames[61] — clarified some — that clarified some of the procedural dimensions of adequate consultation, especially Clyde River, which found some established procedures to be inadequate for this purpose. This is a story that has by no means reached its conclusion, but McLachlin Court decisions will frame its evolution for some considerable time to come.

Another important case, ten years later than Haida Nation, was Tsilhqot'in[62], which revisited and refined the elements of the test for establishing Aboriginal title to land. One of the critical elements involved adjusting previously accepted tests to accommodate the fact that many Indigenous peoples had followed nomadic or semi-nomadic lifestyles, which meant that the earlier tests' emphasis on "regular and exclusive" occupation of land were inappropriate. Most significantly for the Indigenous peoples, the outcome was a complete vindication of their claims, with the decision directly granting "a declaration of Aboriginal title over the area requested" by the Tsilhqot'in. This was the first time that a case of this sort had ended with such an explicit victory.

Daniels v. Canada[63] raised the issue of the meaning of Indians in section 91.24 of the Constitution Act, 1867, which gave the federal government exclusive legislative jurisdiction over "Indians and lands reserved to Indians." Such jurisdiction implied not only legislative authority but also politically relevant obligations, which explains why the federal government was defending a narrow definition of the term.

The question in this case was whether the term included non-status Indians and Métis as well as the long-standing group of "status Indians" created and maintained by the procedures within the *Indian Act*.[64] The end result was a victory, albeit a very partial one, for the two Aboriginal communities involved in the litigation — the Métis and non-status Indians. The court agreed that they were indeed included in federal legislative jurisdiction, but declined to declare either that the Crown owed a fiduciary duty to the two groups or that they had the right to be consulted and negotiated with, on the grounds that such declarations would "lack practical utility."[65] This seems to be at least a partial retreat from the earlier decision in *Manitoba Métis Federation* which had held that the principle of the honour of the Crown (and therefore the duty to consult) did apply to the Manitoba Métis.[66]

FEDERALISM

Co-operative Federalism

Constitutional cases raising federalism issues have been on the rise in the twenty-first century. In deciding these cases, the Court has generally continued its long-term tendency to permit a flexible enforcement of the division of legislative authority. The court has long rejected a "watertight compartments" approach to the division of powers[67] that would move towards a "bright line" division between the legislative activities of the two levels of government, having long since developed several doctrines that permit both levels of government to be active in ways that overlap.[68] The firm test has tended to be "direct conflict," with the application of that term tilted towards the permissive rather than the restrictive. Peter Oliver's concluding comments about the first decade of federalism cases in the McLachlin court characterizes the court as having "continued the trend of upholding legislation" (rather than striking it down on the basis of more restrictive and exclusive approaches), as well as making "important adjustments to constitutional doctrines and methods of analysis to promote this sort of cooperative federalism."[69]

A prime example of this approach can be seen in the *Canadian Western Bank* decision in 2007.[70] Given that insurance regulation has always been accepted as falling under provincial jurisdiction,[71] while the chartered banks are clearly subject to exclusive federal jurisdiction, the issue arose as to who has jurisdiction when the chartered banks expand their services to include some insurance services to their clients. Although the case could have been handled in keeping with a longstanding approach (insurance is not part of the "core element" of banking, which means that the provincial regulations do not impair the actions of a federally regulated service), the Court went further and used the occasion to acknowledge frankly that some matters simply cannot be categorized under one head of power. *Canadian Western Bank* therefore demonstrates that the court is "simply not inclined to put obstacles in the way of federal and provincial legislative intentions."[72]

The *Moloney Trilogy*[73] offers another example of the McLachlin Court's accommodative approach towards both federal and provincial jurisdiction. The cases involved conflicts between the federal government's jurisdiction over bankruptcy and certain provisions of provincial laws regarding specific kinds of debt. In all three cases, both the federal and provincial statutes were upheld as valid legislation. All these judgments were unanimous as to outcome, emphasizing the importance of "co-operative federalism" such that "the principle of [federal] paramountcy must be narrowly construed."

One case stands out against this accommodative tendency, but in a way that supports rather than undermines a very general and gradual drift towards upholding provincial legislative and regulative initiatives in the face of competing federal jurisdiction; that case is the *Securities Reference* decision in 2011.[74] Responding to the global financial crisis of 2008, the federal government contemplated new legislation that would create a single national securities regulator to replace the various provincial regulators that had long been in place. Faced by opposition from several provinces (Alberta, Quebec, Manitoba and New Brunswick), the federal government chose to refer the matter to the Supreme Court, asking for an advisory opinion as to its constitutionality before enacting the legislation. The obvious assumption is that they expected an easy win that would strengthen their hand in these negotiations; that is not how things turned out. The Supreme Court unanimously ruled the proposed legislation unconstitutional. Even though it would only apply to those provinces and territories that chose to opt in, it was still seen as intruding upon the longstanding practice of provincial regulation, without any convincing demonstration of how, why and when securities regulation might have changed in such a way as to make it a matter of genuine national importance and scope. The Court viewed the day-to-day regulation of securities as involving provincial concerns that fell within the "property and civil rights" jurisdiction assigned to the provinces, not something that had risen to the level of national concern. The decision concluded with a very unusual exhortation for honouring the practice of co-operation as the "animating force" of Canadian federalism.

Building on the 2011 decision, the federal government and six provinces constructed a plan for a pan-Canadian securities regulator that would include the provinces that opted in to the plan.[75] This resulted in a reference question on the constitutionality of the new scheme. The Wagner Court in 2018 declared that this co-operative approach was constitutional, commending the co-operative elements and rejecting the argument that they unduly fettered the legislative sovereignty of either level of government.[76]

In the meantime, however, the McLachlin Court had handed down another decision that amply demonstrated both the limits and the problems of co-operative agreements between the two levels of government. The 1995 *Firearms Act* had set up a comprehensive scheme for licensing and registering all firearms in a way that involved the provinces collecting and storing information. When the Harper government abolished the gun registry, it also ordered all data that had been collected under the program to be destroyed. Quebec objected to the destruction of the data relating to the province of Quebec, and it challenged that aspect of the new legislation as violating the principle of co-operative federalism. The Court ruled against the province because the abolition of the registry was governed by exclusive federal jurisdiction over the criminal law.[77] The three Quebec judges jointly wrote a strong dissent in a narrow 5–4 decision.

The McLachlin Court decisions on federal-provincial issues underline the primary challenge of federal-provincial co-operation as a central functioning element of Canadian federalism. Collaborative agreements can be reached on almost any subject, regardless of where it falls within the constitutional division of legislative authority and extensive administrative arrangements can be built around them. However, the principle of legislative sovereignty means that any such agreement can be ended unilaterally and sometimes abruptly.

National Institutions

The general tendency of a mildly province-favouring doctrine of accommodative federalism can be seen in two very high-profile decisions about the reform of national institutions. On its face, the constitutional amendment process constrains both levels of government. But when we are speaking of changes to national institutions, the result again enhances a notion of federalism that emphasizes the roles and powers of provincial governments, the more so as both decisions were responses to recent initiatives of the federal government.

The *Senate Reference* (2014)[78]

The Supreme Court's decision clarifying the nature of Canada's Senate in 2014 paved the way for the appointment of independent senators beginning in 2015. This decision of a Supreme Court headed by McLachlin — a judge from western Canada — helped to resolve, at least for a time, a debate about Senate reform that began in western Canada in the 1980s.[79]

The Senate is one of two chambers of Canada's Parliament. Up to 2015, senators had been appointed by the party in power in large measure for patronage or partisan reasons. As a result, the Senate was largely unable to fulfill its original purpose — a chamber of nonpartisan, sober second thought that also ensured adequate regional representation that might not result from a general election for the House of Commons.

In 2013, Stephen Harper's government introduced legislation that would permit senator-in-waiting elections in all provinces and territories, and would introduce term limits for senators. Because of widespread concern that the legislation was unconstitutional,[80] the government sent a reference question to the Supreme Court asking several questions related to Senate reform.

In answering these questions, the unanimous McLachlin Court in 2014 held that a constitutional amendment supported by Parliament and seven of ten provincial legislatures would be required to change the Senate from an appointed to an elected body. The judges also held that abolition of the Senate would require a constitutional amendment approved by Parliament and all provincial legislatures.[81]

The Supreme Court's reasoning was that an appointed Senate, in which senators hold office until retirement, is part of Canada's "constitutional architecture."[82] In the negotiations leading up to Confederation in 1867, according to evidence presented to the Court, the nature of the upper house in the new Parliament was of paramount importance, and the union would never have come about without agreement about the Senate. Lower Canada (Quebec) saw the proposed Senate as a means to protect French language rights, and the maritime provinces saw it as a place to safeguard minority religious rights and regional interests. The Senate was to be appointed rather than elected so that it could act as a nonpartisan chamber of sober second thought. Senators were appointed for life (after 1965, until retirement at age seventy-five) to encourage independent legislative review based on years of experience. According to the McLachlin Court:

The contrast between election for members of the House of Commons and executive appointment for Senators is not an accident of history. The framers of the Constitution Act, 1867 *deliberately chose executive appointment of Senators in order to allow the Senate to play the specific role of a complementary legislative body of "sober second thought."*[83]

The judges also quoted from a 1980 Supreme Court decision about the Senate:

As this Court wrote in the Upper House Reference, "[i]n creating the Senate in the manner provided in the Act, *it is clear that the intention was to make the Senate a thoroughly independent body which could* canvass dispassionately the measures of the House of Commons." [emphasis added][84]

The court observed,

The framers sought to endow the Senate with independence from the electoral process to which members of the House of Commons were subject, in order to remove Senators from a partisan political arena that required unremitting consideration of short-term political objectives.[85]

The McLachlin Court's 2014 decision on Senate reform not only settled the question about whether Parliament could unilaterally make the Senate an elected body, but also reminded Canadians about the intense debates concerning the Senate that led to Confederation in 1867. The Senate was envisioned as an essential institution that could both counterbalance potential dominance by the most populous regions and provide a setting for dispassionate review of legislation from the elected chamber that is sometimes tainted by partisanship and "short-term political objectives." It also laid to rest proposals to abolish the Senate.[86] The Liberal government elected in 2015 created an independent advisory board for selecting and appointing nonpartisan, independent senators.[87] As of 2019, the majority of senators are independent. Polls report strong support for the new system from the Canadian public.[88]

The abandonment of party affiliation as the vehicle for Senate appointments and the movement towards a nonpartisan system represent the most important change in the institutional features of the Canadian system of government since the 1982 amendments to the Constitution, which resulted in the *Charter of Rights* and the made-in-Canada constitutional amendment formula.

The Supreme Court Reference (2014)[89]

Earlier in 2014, proposed minor changes to the Supreme Court itself had been the subject of another reference case.[90] The case involved the Harper government's appointment of Marc Nadon to the Supreme Court, but the case addressed broader questions as well. There were several sections of the *Supreme Court Act* that applied only to Quebec. The reference asked primarily about the interpretation and application of these sections. Just in case the Court interpreted these sections narrowly, the government had introduced amendments to the *Supreme Court Act* that would have removed the problem, and the constitutionality of those changes was also at issue.

In addition, this decision finally addressed an ambiguous feature of the 1982 constitutional changes. On the one hand, the constitutional amendment provisions specifically applying to the Supreme Court required some level of federal-provincial agreement; on the other hand, these provisions applied to "changes to the Constitution of Canada" and, curiously, the *Supreme Court Act* was not among those federal statutes that were listed as forming part of the written Constitution.[91] The Supreme Court's decision clarified that changes to the essential features of the Supreme Court would require federal-provincial agreement, on the grounds that the Supreme Court had evolved into a central feature of Canada's "constitutional architecture."[92] That being the case, the Harper government's attempted amendments to the *Supreme Court Act* were ruled unconstitutional.

The decision of the McLachlin majority emphasizes the "historic bargain that gave birth to the Court in 1875."[93] Quebec has a unique legal system in Canada that is based in part on French civil law. Quebec only agreed to the creation of the Supreme Court on the condition that there would a group of Quebec judges on the Court who would be qualified to make decisions about Quebec civil law that were credible in the eyes of Quebeckers. Those qualifications were stated in the *Supreme Court Act*, and the McLachlin majority decided that the interpretation of these provisions should be strict because of the importance of the "bargain."

More generally, this pair of decisions delivered the message that the federal government's ability to make changes unilaterally to national institutions was extremely constrained, rather more so than many had thought before these decisions were handed down. The flip side of these decisions is that the capacity of provincial governments was enhanced by the fact that the formal constitutional amendment process, with all its practical difficulties, is now required for changes to essential features of the Senate and the Supreme Court.

"Free Trade" Between the Provinces

The federalism story of the McLachlin Court jurisprudence culminates in *Comeau*, the "free the beer" case.[94] The immediate facts were straightforward. The government of New Brunswick, like that of other provinces, strictly limits the quantities of liquor that can be brought in from other provinces, the effect being to create a legally enforceable monopoly for the New Brunswick Liquor Corporation. Given that prices in Quebec were lower, people who lived close to the border often slipped into Quebec for their liquor purchases, and the New Brunswick police were directed to discourage this by imposing the relevant fines. Gerard Comeau was one of the individuals involved, and he chose to defend himself on constitutional grounds, taking the case all the way to the Supreme Court.

At issue was section 121 of the *Constitution Act, 1867*, which provides that "all Articles of the Growth, Produce or Manufacture of any one of the provinces shall, from and after the Union, be admitted free into each of the other Provinces." Comeau's argument was that New Brunswick's regulations and fines violated this provision.

Although the initial trial judge accepted the argument, a unanimous nine-judge Supreme Court panel went the other way. Not only did the Court uphold the decades-old practice dating from the 1921 precedent establishing a very narrow reading of section 121 on the grounds that the New Brunswick regulations were aimed at protecting the health and well-being of people in the province, and only incidentally affected interprovincial trade, but it ramped up the rhetoric in such a way that many commentators have described it as effectively gutting section 121.

The real issue is not "free the beer" so much as "lower the barriers to interprovincial trade." The Court acknowledged that it was being invited to overturn an old precedent, but it ruled that there were no new legal issues, significant developments or sufficient evidence to justify upsetting long-settled law. This decision amounts to a dramatic affirmation of provincial jurisdiction in what has been a hotly contested aspect of federalism and the Canadian economy.

ADMINISTRATIVE LAW

The McLachlin Court decision with the greatest lasting impact may not be a constitutional decision at all, but rather one that deals with administrative law, and focuses on what must, at first glance, look like a narrowly technical question pertaining to "standards of

review."[95] The case was *Dunsmuir*[96] and the debate about its usefulness and appropriateness has raged for more than a decade, even as
the string of subsequent and related decisions grows steadily.

The central issue regarding standards of review is the interaction between the courts on one hand and the plethora of modern
administrative boards and agencies on the other. The modern
administrative state relies increasingly on these sorts of bodies,
and they exercise authority over an enormous range of activities
by both private and public actors in a way that constantly engages
the fuzzy boundary between "administrative" and "judicial" action.
Given the very broad extent of their reach, exempting them
from judicial review of their decisions and procedures would be
unthinkable, but simply treating them as if they were lower courts
with the legal professionalism and formal procedures this implies
would be unworkable. Hence the "standards of review" question.

Judicial review of a decision by an administrator or administrative tribunal does not involve asking a court to go through the
whole process all over again (de novo review) and reach its own
independent decision. Rather, the application for judicial review
must be based on the argument that the administrative decision
maker or tribunal actually made a mistake, and that the court
should "fix" the mistake by changing the decision or sending it
back for reconsideration. It is not even enough for the judges on
the higher court to think that they might have decided the case differently. They must take the further step of deciding that the initial
decision was outside the range of the reasonable and permissible,
and beyond the appropriate discretion of the decision maker.

But there is a further aspect of the "standards of review" problem for administrative boards and tribunals. The whole point of
establishing these bodies was to draw upon a particular type of
experience and expertise, and to allow them to operate in ways that
differ from the full procedural rigour of the superior courts. Apart
from a concern with protecting the "core" jurisdiction of the provincial superior courts,[97] the leading case in relation to the board/

court interface up to *Dunsmuir* was the Laskin Court's decision in *CUPE v. New Brunswick*[98] in 1979, and there was some concern that judicial doctrine was being left behind by the ongoing development of the administrative state.

Dunsmuir was the court's ambitious attempt to resolve this issue. Its central thrust was greater deference to decisions of these boards, especially regarding their own "home" statute and especially when the issues involved were closely related to their expertise. Controversially, later decisions have extended this deference to the boards' findings on their own constitutionality and limitations, and to decisions with fragmentary or incomplete reasons.[99]

At the same time, the Court has decided that when the actions of boards are challenged under the *Charter*, they should be assessed under a more relaxed standard than that established in the longstanding *Oakes* decision, which outlined the standard for deciding whether provincial or federal statutes constitute "reasonable limits" under section 1 of the *Charter*. The new test for administrative boards is "a robust proportionality analysis consistent with administrative law principles" rather than a formal section 1 analysis.[100]

As well, the Court has taken very seriously the broad statutory purposes often assigned to boards, even to the extent of overriding explicit legislative provisions that would at first glance operate to contain them.[101] More recently, it has upheld the specialized expertise of a regulatory body even when the decision in question was reached by a referendum vote from a much wider membership body.[102]

Quite apart from the fact that the vagueness of many of these evolving rules makes court decisions harder to anticipate, there is a deeper concern about the pronounced decrease in the success of court challenges to the decisions or procedures of administrative boards.[103] If the purpose of the *Charter* is to protect citizen rights against government action, and if much government action is carried on through administrative boards and agencies, this permissiveness has very serious implications. Commentary in law journals and law blogs repeatedly heralds an upcoming case as an opportunity for a major rethink of *Dunsmuir*, only to be just as repeatedly disappointed. Whatever the long-term evolution of judicial doctrine on this subject, whatever the outcome of the controversy it has generated,[104] it is clear that this case will remain a major element of the McLachlin court's legacy.

THE IMPACT OF THE McLACHLIN COURT
Overall, the legacy of the McLachlin court's jurisprudence can be summarized as a robust application of the right to security of the person, an advancement of the rights of labour unions and Indigenous peoples, a clarification of the constitutional status of the Senate and the Supreme Court of Canada, and a softening of judicial scrutiny over administrative tribunals.

6

McLachlin's Leading Decisions as Chief Justice

In a year-end editorial in December 2018, *The Globe and Mail* celebrated the virtue of the concept of reasonableness in Canada.[1] It referred to the principle of the "reasonable person" developed in Canadian jurisprudence and applied to the resolution of difficult issues. The editorial evoked the danger posed by unreasoned and simplistic approaches to public policy determined primarily by political or ideological agendas: "Without lots of reasonable persons, among both the electorate and the elected, democratic politics goes off the rails."[2]

Beverley McLachlin, we argue, is a beacon of this quality. Her decisions are evidence-based, thorough and sensible. Her opinions, individually or in concert with the court, demonstrate concern for some of the most vulnerable in society — those suffering from terminal and debilitating illnesses, prostitutes, prisoners and suspected security threats. Some may find her conclusions unexpected, but her pragmatic reasoning is persuasive.

This chapter reviews McLachlin's decisions in a dozen Supreme

Court cases which have had an impact on the lives of Canadians, and Canadian public policy, after McLachlin became chief justice in 2000. The cases selected represent a small fraction of the hundreds of Supreme Court decisions that McLachlin participated in during that time, and we leave out decisions that are of great interest to lawyers but not necessarily the general public. As a result, the majority of decisions examined here are about the *Charter of Rights* and Aboriginal rights.

In addition to decisions that McLachlin has authored, some of the decisions referred to below are decisions that McLachlin co-authored with one or more other judges, and some are unanimous decisions of the McLachlin Court. McLachlin has a distinctive writing style relating to logic, organization and clarity. The "for the court" or co-authored decisions that McLachlin participated in that we discuss in this chapter all bear heavy imprints of McLachlin's approach.[3]

LEGAL RIGHTS DECISIONS

Dying with Dignity: *Carter* (2015)[4]

In 2015, a unanimous Supreme Court struck down the *Criminal Code* provision that had prohibited anyone from assisting a terminally ill person to end his or her life. In doing so, the Court overruled its 1993 decision in the *Sue Rodriguez* case that upheld this *Criminal Code* prohibition (and in which, as noted earlier, McLachlin had dissented).

In the 2015 *Carter* case, McLachlin's Court considered a new challenge to the prohibition of assisted suicide brought by Lee Carter, her husband Hollis Johnson and others. Lee Carter's eighty-nine-year-old mother, Kay Carter, was suffering from spinal stenosis, which "left her dependent on others to eat, get dressed, go to the bathroom — she couldn't even rise from a chair or bed without assistance. She didn't want to live that way and she wanted to leave life on her own terms."[5] Lee and Hollis helped Kay to end her life, at Kay's request, in Switzerland, where physician-assisted suicide was legal. Lee Carter and Hollis Johnson joined litigation initiated by the B.C. Civil Liberties Association. When the case reached the Supreme Court in 2015, the unanimous decision attributed to the Court struck down the *Criminal Code* prohibition.

The Court's majority in the 1993 *Rodriguez* case was concerned about leaving the door open to mistreatment of vulnerable persons. In *Carter*, the judges wrote that during the twenty-two years since the *Rodriguez* case, there had been ample evidence collected from jurisdictions where assisted suicide was legal to show that procedures designed to protect the vulnerable can work.

In the *Carter* decision, the Court concluded,

> *The prohibition on physician-assisted dying is void insofar as it deprives a competent adult of such assistance where (1) the person affected clearly consents to the termination of life; and (2) the person has a grievous and irremediable medical condition (including an illness, disease or disability) that causes enduring suffering that is intolerable to the individual in the circumstances of his or her condition.*[6]

In a comment in 2017 about the dying with dignity issue, McLachlin said, "It's hard just to overlook that suffering."[7]

After approving an extension, the Court gave Parliament until June 2016 to enact legislation that would permit assisted suicide, and also meet the safeguards that the court had outlined in its decision. Legislation was enacted in June 2016 that made physician-assisted suicide legal, under stringent conditions. To qualify for assisted death, a patient requesting it must have an incurable and irremediable medical condition that is in irreversible decline, and that patient's natural death must be reasonably foreseeable. Assisted death is not available to those with a curable condition, or to minors, to those with a long-term disability or on the basis of mental illness.

McLachlin's dissent in *Rodriguez* and her decision as part of a unanimous court in *Carter* demonstrate both a strict rule-of-law approach towards the application of the section 7 right to security of the person and empathy with those whose suffering is irreversible. The volumes of research presented in the *Carter* case about assisted-death procedures in jurisdictions outside Canada brought unanimity to the Court.

Prostitution: *Bedford* (2013)

Prostitution has never been illegal in Canada, but Canada's *Criminal Code* has made some activities associated with prostitution illegal to discourage the practice.[8] In 1983, the Mulroney government amended the *Criminal Code* to make it illegal to communicate in a public place for the purposes of prostitution. This legislation was challenged in court as a violation of the right to freedom of expression. In 1990, a Supreme Court majority found that this provision was constitutional. The Court held that although the provision violated freedom of expression, it was a reasonable limit in that it supported the important objective of deterring prostitution.[9]

Little social science evidence about the impact of the 1983 *Criminal Code* provision prohibiting communication for the purposes of prostitution was available to the Supreme Court in 1990. After 1990, studies were conducted that indicated that the *Criminal Code*'s communication provision was forcing prostitutes into dangerous surroundings so that they would not be caught communicating. In 2007, Robert Pickton was convicted of murdering six prostitutes, though he likely killed as many as sixty.[10] The publicity surrounding the Pickton case drew attention to the dangers faced by prostitutes under the 1983 legislation.

In 2008, Terri Jean Bedford, along with Amy Lebovitch and Valerie Scott, went to court to challenge the 1983 legislation and two related *Criminal Code* provisions,[11] given new social science evidence that they argued proved that the *Criminal Code* provision regarding communication violated the rights to life and security of the person in section 7 of the *Charter*. They filed eighty-eight volumes (25,000 pages) of evidence in the Superior Court of Ontario. The trial judge ruled in their favour, as did the Ontario Court of Appeal in 2012. At the Supreme Court level, Beverley McLachlin delivered the unanimous judgment of the nine-judge panel in Bedford's favour. She wrote that the purpose of the 1983 legislation was to prevent public nuisance. On the basis of the evidence presented, the three provisions of the *Criminal Code* related to prostitution were "arbitrary, overbroad or grossly disproportionate"[12] to the objective of the legislation:

> *The prohibitions at issue do not merely impose conditions on how prostitutes operate. They go a critical step further, by imposing dangerous conditions on prostitution; they prevent people engaged in a risky — but legal — activity from taking steps to protect themselves from the risks . . . The bawdy-house prohibition prevents resort to safe houses, to which prostitutes working on the street can take clients. In Vancouver, for example, "Grandma's House" was established to support street workers in the Downtown Eastside at about the same time as fears were growing that a serial killer was prowling the streets — fears which materialized in the notorious Robert Pickton. Street prostitutes — who the application judge found are largely the most vulnerable class of prostitutes, and who face an alarming amount of violence . . . were able to bring clients to Grandma's House. However, charges were laid . . . [and] Grandma's House was shut down.*[13]

The government had argued that the Court ought to defer to parliamentary legislation about such a complex social issue, but

McLachlin countered that deference is not appropriate when it leads to "harmful effects [that] . . . negatively impact security of the person under s. 7 of the *Charter*."[14] The declaration of invalidity of the three *Criminal Code* provisions was suspended for one year so that Parliament could find an appropriate remedy that did not violate *Charter* protections.[15] The legislative response by the Harper government was to make the purchase of sex illegal, while not criminalizing the sale of sex by adults. No doubt, the constitutionality of this legislation will be challenged again in the Wagner Court.

Harm Reduction: *Insite* (2012)

Thousands of drug addicts live in Vancouver's Downtown Eastside, one of Canada's poorest neighbourhoods. In the 1990s, this area was home to more than 4,600 intravenous drug users, many of whom became infected with hepatitis C or HIV, and annual deaths from overdoses were in the hundreds.[16] Action needed to be taken. A coalition of stakeholders came together to develop a plan for Canada's first safe injection site, which became known as Insite. The plan's backers included a nonprofit organization serving Downtown Eastside residents, along with city council, the mayor, the premier, the police, former premiers and mayors, unions, the International AIDS Society and merchants' associations.

The Insite safe injection site, which opened in 2003, did not provide illegal drugs. It offered a safe place for drug addicts to use their substances with clean needles. It was located in the same building as a treatment facility where drug users were encouraged to begin the process of overcoming their addictions and regaining their health. From the beginning, data were collected so that Insite could be properly evaluated according to social science standards.

For Insite to operate, it required an exemption from the federal *Controlled Drugs and Substances Act* so that those using the facility would not be arrested. In 2003, when the Liberal Party was in power, Insite received a five-year exemption from Canada's minister of health. By 2008, evaluations of Insite showed that it helped addicts to recover, prevented deaths and significantly reduced the number of those infected with hepatitis C and HIV. In spite of this evidence, Tony Clement, the minister of health in Stephen Harper's Conservative government, refused to continue Insite's exemption. Two nonprofits and two Insite clients went to court to try to keep Insite open, and their case reached the Supreme Court in 2011.[17]

The unanimous decision of the full nine-judge court was written by Beverley McLachlin. She wrote that section 7 of the *Charter of Rights* guarantees the right to life and security of the person, unless these rights are properly limited according to fundamental justice. Clement's refusal to continue the exemption, in the light of evidence that Insite saved lives and improved health, was arbitrary:

> *Insite has been proven to save lives with no discernable negative impact on the public safety and health objectives of Canada. The effect of denying the services of Insite to the population it serves and the correlative increase in the risk of death and disease to injection drug users is grossly disproportionate to any benefit that Canada might derive from presenting a uniform stance on the possession of narcotics.*[18]

The minister of health was ordered to grant the exemption.

In her decision, McLachlin set strict limits for future safe injection sites like Insite. There would need to be broad stakeholder support for such a facility, as there was for Insite, and properly collected data would need to show conclusively that lives were being saved and health was being improved for exemptions to receive *Charter* protection.

Fair Treatment for al Qaeda Detainees: The *Khadr* Decisions (2008 and 2010)[19]

In 2002, Omar Khadr, a fifteen-year-old Canadian, was forced by his father — an ardent al Qaeda supporter — to fight for al Qaeda in Afghanistan. Khadr was captured by U.S. forces, accused of killing a U.S. soldier and taken to the U.S. detention camp in Guantánamo Bay, Cuba. (According to the Child Soldier Treaty that Canada has signed on to, Khadr was a child soldier entitled to rehabilitation treatment, but the United States was not a party to that treaty.) There was evidence that U.S. authorities tortured Khadr on a number of occasions to try to obtain intelligence information. He was interviewed by Canadian officials twice, in 2003 and 2004, at Guantánamo Bay. He was denied legal counsel for the first interview, and he had been deprived of sleep for three weeks prior to the second. The Canadian officials knew this and also knew that the evidence they gathered from the interviews would be used against Khadr in military hearings in Guantánamo Bay that did not include the usual rule-of-law safeguards for accused persons.[20]

Khadr requested a copy of the transcripts of the interviews with the Canadian officials and was refused. In 2005, he applied for a court order for disclosure of the transcripts in Canada's Federal Court, and the case ended up in the Supreme Court in 2008. A unanimous decision was issued, attributed to the Court. The decision concluded that because of the clear violations of Khadr's *Charter* rights by Canadian officials,

> *The principles of international law and comity of nations, which normally require that Canadian officials operating abroad comply with local law, do not extend to participation in processes that violate Canada's international human rights obligations.*[21]

In situations of extreme human rights violations, the Canadian *Charter of Rights and Freedoms* applies to the actions of Canadian officials abroad. As a result, the Court ordered that a Federal Court judge review the transcripts of the interviews, and after hearing from lawyers for Khadr and the Canadian government, disclose to Khadr all documents that are not a risk to national security.[22]

In 2008, a House of Commons subcommittee on international human rights considered the Khadr situation. It recommended that Canada meet its obligations under the Child Soldier Treaty by requesting Khadr's repatriation from Guantánamo Bay so that he could be dealt with under Canadian law.[23] At that point, Khadr was the only foreign national still held in Guantánamo Bay.[24]

Khadr's lawyers applied to Federal Court for an order to compel the Canadian government to request Khadr's repatriation to be dealt with by Canadian law. The Federal Court made such an order, but McLachlin's Supreme Court was not willing to go that far. In 2010, the Supreme Court decision first affirmed the seriousness of the violations of Khadr's *Charter* rights by Canadian officials:

> *Interrogation of a youth, to elicit statements about the most serious criminal charges while detained in these conditions and without access to counsel, and while knowing that the fruits of the interrogations would be shared with the U.S. prosecutors, offends the most basic Canadian standards about the treatment of detained youth suspects.*[25]

However, the court stopped short of ordering Khadr's repatriation. After declaring that Khadr's *Charter* rights had been violated, the McLachlin Court wrote, in an exercise of judicial restraint, that it was up to the Canadian government to determine the appropriate remedy.

In spite of the Court's strongly worded decision, the government refused to repatriate Khadr, requesting instead that the United States treat Khadr fairly according to international standards.

However, U.S. officials in Guantánamo continued to prosecute Khadr in violation of rule-of-law standards in the continental United States and Canada.

In 2010, Khadr was given two options. He could plead not guilty to the charges against him, in which case he would almost surely be found guilty in an illegal court that accepted tainted evidence and sentenced to life imprisonment in Guantánamo. Alternatively, he could plead guilty, and in return receive an eight-year sentence along with a commitment from U.S. officials to return him to Canada. Khadr had no real choice. He pleaded guilty and returned to Canada in 2012. He spent three years in Canadian prisons and then was released in 2015, given the likely success of an appeal of his Guantánamo conviction in the continental United States.

The two unanimous Khadr decisions provide a clear illustration of the strict rule-of-law approach the McLachlin Court took when in collision with a government willing to tolerate arbitrary procedures. However, the 2010 decision indicates judicial deference to the government's prerogative to find a remedy.

RIGHTS OF INDIGENOUS PEOPLES

Haida Nation (2004)[26]

The *Haida Nation* case was the first major Indigenous case to reach the Supreme Court after Beverley McLachlin became chief justice. McLachlin wrote the decision for a unanimous seven-judge panel. The issue was whether non-Indigenous development can take place on lands to which First Nations groups had strong claims but regarding which there had as yet been no land claims settlement.

For centuries, the Haida Nation has inhabited Haida Gwaii, an archipelago west of the B.C. mainland that is twice the size of Prince Edward Island. Since the early twentieth century, the Haida Nation has claimed title, but it was only after section 35 became part of the Canadian Constitution in 1982 that the Haida Nation had the opportunity to litigate with any reasonable chance of success.

In the 1990s, the government of British Columbia issued permits for the Weyerhaeuser timber company to harvest forests on Haida Gwaii, and in 2000 the Haida Nation went to court to seek a declaration that the permits were illegal without their consent. McLachlin noted that the government of B.C. held legal title to the land on which the permits were issued, but the Haida people were in the process of trying to prove a title claim.[27] As a result, the B.C. government had a duty to consult in good faith with the Haida people about the harvest of timber. Such consultation "may in turn lead to an obligation to accommodate Haida concerns in the harvesting of timber, although what accommodation if any may be required cannot at this time be ascertained. Consultation must be meaningful."[28]

This decision has encouraged both negotiation and litigation between Haida representatives and the federal and provincial governments. Some small progress has been made up to 2019, though rebuilding trust between the Haida people and various levels of government may take decades.[29]

Tsilhqot'in Nation and Grassy Narrows (2014)[30]

Two Aboriginal rights decisions penned by Beverley McLachlin in 2014, two weeks apart, represent her most forceful decisions in support of First Nations claims. Previous Supreme Court decisions from *Delgamuukw* to *Haida Nation* emphasized the need for negotiations about land claims, and the Supreme Court provided guidelines for discussions. In the 2014 decisions, McLachlin and her colleagues were prepared to impose solutions.

In 1983, the B.C. government granted a logging permit to a company to harvest trees in an area of 1,900 square kilometres in central B.C. claimed by the Tsilhqot'in.[31] The Tsilhqot'in objected and organized blockades of the logging roads. Litigation and negotiation ensued until 2002, when a trial over the Tsilhqot'in land claim began that lasted 339 days over five years. The trial judge ruled in 2007 that the Tsilhqot'in were entitled to a declaration of Aboriginal title in principle. However, in 2012 the B.C. Court of Appeal ruled that the claim had not yet been established, though it might in the future. The Tsilhqot'in appealed that decision to the Supreme Court of Canada and won.

McLachlin conceded that the evidence was complex. The Tsilhqot'in had been a semi-nomadic Indigenous group, and the B.C. Court of Appeal would have restricted the claim to the villages that the Tsilhqot'in had most recently occupied. However, McLachlin wrote that there was enough evidence to show that the Tsilhqot'in had occupied the claimed area for centuries, and this occupation was "exclusive" in the sense that other tribes required permission from the Tsilhqot'in to enter the area. Rather than send the claim back to another trial or more negotiations, McLachlin declared that the trial judge had been right in 2007. He had canvassed the evidence thoroughly, had "spent time in the claim area, and heard extensive evidence from elders, historians, and other experts."[32] No more delay would be tolerated.

With regard to the logging operations, there was no evidence that the B.C. government had made any attempt to consult the Tsilhqot'in or accommodate their concerns. The B.C. government claimed that it could not consult because of an emergency pine-beetle infestation and the importance of the economic benefits to the province. McLachlin wrote that there was no compelling evidence for either.

Both where an unsettled land claim is strong, and where Aboriginal title has been established, the government has a duty to consult.[33] Failure to consult will create a liability for the government or for the private interests involved. Ignoring the duty to consult could result in a government being "charged with" failure to adequately consult.[34]

The *Grassy Narrows* decision also concerned adequate consultation with First Nations regarding timber rights, although the major issue was about whether the federal or Ontario government was obligated to honour Indigenous treaty and related rights.

In 1912, a large area near the Grassy Narrows reserve in Ontario, on which the band had harvesting timber rights, was ceded to the Ontario government by the government of Canada. In 1997, the Ontario government authorized a pulp and paper company to clearcut a large area of land in the area where the Grassy Narrows band had harvesting rights. There had been no consultation with the band. McLachlin wrote that the Ontario government, not the federal government, had the duty to manage these lands while taking into account the interests of the Grassy Narrows band. Care had to be taken to ensure that there would be meaningful, good-faith consultation with the band, and that commercial development would not unnecessarily interfere with the band's harvesting rights.[35]

Ktunaxa Nation v. British Columbia[36]

The last major case about Aboriginal rights that McLachlin took part in was *Ktunaxa Nation*. The case concerned both the B.C. government's duty to consult about the use of land subject to an Indigenous land claim, and freedom of religion under the *Charter*.

The Jumbo Mountain area about sixty kilometres west of Invermere in southeastern B.C. is home to four large high-altitude glaciers located on B.C. Crown land that can accommodate skiing twelve months a year. A resort company began to negotiate with the B.C. government in the early 1990s for permission to build a major ski resort there, and the negotiations included consultations with the Ktunaxa because of a potential land claim.

Some changes were made to the resort's plans to accommodate the Ktunaxa, but late in the negotiation process the Ktunaxa argued that the proposed ski resort would result in irreparable damage to their religious beliefs. They claimed that the Jumbo Mountain area was home to the Grizzly Bear Spirit which is sacred to the Ktunaxa, and the resort would drive the spirit away. In 2012, the government approved the development, and the Ktunaxa initiated litigation to stop it.

The Supreme Court was unanimous in dismissing the Ktunaxa claim. All nine judges agreed that there had been sufficient
consultation with the Ktunaxa and good-faith attempts to
accommodate their concerns. McLachlin and Malcolm Rowe
wrote a decision for themselves and five other judges which
concluded that approval of the resort did not violate freedom
of religion, because the approval does not interfere with "the
freedom to hold a religious belief or to manifest that belief."[37]
Michael Moldaver wrote a separate concurring decision for
himself and Suzanne Côté in which he claimed that there had
been a violation of freedom of religion because the resort would
render the Jumbo Mountain area "devoid of any spiritual significance." Nevertheless, Moldaver concluded that, on balance,
the accommodation that the government had made with the
Ktunaxa in other ways was "proportionately balanced."[38]

After First Nations had achieved some important victories in the
McLachlin Court, *Ktunaxa* was a clear setback, especially McLachlin's relatively narrow interpretation of freedom of religion.

McLachlin's contribution to Aboriginal rights cases illustrates a rule-of-law approach that does not tolerate arbitrary
limits on First Nations' rights. In a speech McLachlin gave in
May 2015, she stated that in the early years of Confederation, it
was federal government policy to destroy First Nations cultures,
which she referred to as "cultural genocide."[39] Subsequently,
some of McLachlin's critics accused her of bias towards First
Nations perspectives. However, given the clear evidence that
in its early years the Canadian government had indeed tried
to eradicate First Nations cultures, we see her comments as a
summary of relevant facts rather than bias. Her decisions on
Aboriginal rights show that she has the ability to sort through
large volumes of complex evidence and decide on its credibility
— sometimes in support of First Nations claims, and sometimes
not.[40]

PRISONERS' VOTING RIGHTS

Sauvé (2002)

So far we have seen McLachlin's imprint on Canada's electoral democracy as an associate justice through the *Saskatchewan Electoral Boundaries* decision and her participation in the *Quebec Secession Reference*. After becoming chief justice, she continued to contribute to clarifying the fundamental principles of Canadian democracy in her decision that gave prisoners the right to vote.

There has long been a question about whether prisoners should be able to vote in federal, provincial and municipal elections. The two issues at play here involve assessing the potential good or harm of allowing prisoners to vote and deciding whether the *Charter of Rights* mandates that prisoners have a right to vote.

In the early 2000s, there were approximately 25,000 inmates in provincial jails across Canada, where they were serving sentences of less than two years.[41] Half of these had not been convicted and were simply waiting for a trial. There are fewer than 15,000 inmates in federal penitentiaries, where they are generally serving sentences of more than two years. Some prisoners are on parole. Nearly all of these inmates will eventually be released and reintegrated into Canadian society.

Prior to the *Charter*, Quebec allowed prisoners in provincial jails to vote in Quebec elections, and those on parole from provincial jails across Canada could vote in provincial elections. Those serving time in either federal or provincial jails were not allowed to vote in federal elections even if on parole, according to the *Canada Elections Act*. All this changed as a result of litigation initiated by Richard Sauvé.

Sauvé was convicted of first-degree murder in 1978. He has always claimed his innocence and stated that he was simply in the wrong place at the wrong time. Once he adjusted to prison life, he took advantage of educational opportunities that were available. He eventually earned a BA while in prison and then began work on a master's degree in criminology. He learned that section 3 of the

Charter of Rights guarantees the right of every citizen to vote. As a citizen, he wanted to vote, in part to help promote the improvement of a criminal justice system that he thought had failed him.

In 1988, Sauvé found a lawyer who went to court on his behalf to challenge the denial of prisoners' voting rights in the *Canada Elections Act*. That case ended up in the Supreme Court in 1993, where the court affirmed that the blanket denial of the vote to all prisoners was overbroad.[42] As a result, the federal government amended the *Canada Elections Act* to allow all those serving two years or less to vote. This change did not help Sauvé, as he was serving a longer sentence, so he went to court again. His case reached the Supreme Court of Canada in 2002.

The court's majority decision in favour of Sauvé was written by Beverley McLachlin.[43] She wrote that the denial of the vote to prisoners is a clear violation of section 3. Prisoners who are citizens have a right to vote unless the government can demonstrate that limiting that right is reasonable in a free and democratic society, as permitted by section 1 of the *Charter*.[44]

McLachlin noted that the ultimate objective of imprisonment is the rehabilitation and reintegration of prisoners, and there was no evidence that preventing prisoners from voting would help to rehabilitate them. However, there was persuasive evidence from jurisdictions that allowed prisoners to vote that becoming engaged in the electoral process helped to promote rehabilitation. McLachlin also stated that preventing prisoners from voting would have a disproportionately negative impact on Indigenous peoples because of the disproportionate number of prisoners who are members of Canada's Indigenous population.

Richard Sauvé was granted day release from prison in 1995 and full release on parole in 2002. He apprenticed as a carpenter and then became a child and youth worker. He has worked for or volunteered with several organizations that help prisoners transition to productive lives. He has voted in every election after winning the right to vote.[45]

EQUALITY RIGHTS

Gosselin (2002), *Kapp* (2008) and *Centrale des Syndicats du Québec* (2018)

Soon after becoming chief justice in 2000, McLachlin gave a talk at Osgoode Hall Law School, in which she discussed the challenges of interpreting section 15, the equality provision in the *Charter*, which she said was the hardest section of the *Charter* to interpret.[46] In spite of this difficulty, McLachlin sought to untangle the knots which the Supreme Court has tied itself in when trying to create a consistent framework for section 15 analysis.

As seen earlier, for a decade up to 1999, the test for equality rights violations applied by the Supreme Court of Canada was set out in the 1989 *Andrews* decision.[47] Mark David Andrews had completed all the requirements to become a lawyer except for Canadian citizenship, for which he had to wait the required period. The Supreme Court ruled that the citizenship requirement in this case was both unnecessary and discriminatory and therefore constituted a violation of equality.

According to the *Andrews* test, it is unconstitutional to discriminate on the basis of irrelevant personal characteristics — race, national or ethnic origin, colour, religion, sex, age and mental or physical disability — and categories analogous to these. Persons in these categories are considered discriminated against if they are denied benefits or subjected to disadvantages as a result. There is a *Charter* violation unless the government can prove that this discrimination is a reasonable limit in the context of democratic norms.

In 1999, the *Andrews* test was revised in a decision written by Justice Iacobucci, known as *Law*,[48] which McLachlin signed on to. Nancy Law was left widowed at thirty years old and challenged in court the Canada Pension Plan provision that restricted survivor benefits to spouses over thirty-five. Iacobucci's opinion in *Law* supplemented the *Andrews* standard by creating a complex set of new tests for judges to apply when deciding whether the equality rights section of the *Charter of Rights*, section 15, had been violated by government legislation.

In 2002, McLachlin applied the *Law* test in a case known as *Gosselin* involving Quebec legislation that denied social welfare benefits to Quebec residents under thirty who declined to participate in educational or work experience programs. She wrote that the legislation did not result in discrimination as the legislation was intended to help those under thirty to improve their life prospects, and so was not designed to disadvantage them.[49] This decision disappointed some social activists who had hoped that the Supreme Court would pave the way for broader social welfare supports. For McLachlin, the evidence of discrimination and harm resulting from the legislation was insufficient, and so deference to the Quebec legislation was the right solution.

By the late 2000s, it was evident that the *Law* test of 1999 had not helped because of its complexity. In 2008, McLachlin had the opportunity to help rectify this situation in the *Kapp* decision.[50] The case was launched in response to the Canadian government giving First Nations fishers a one-day monopoly in a B.C. fishing zone to compensate for past violations of treaties involving First Nations fishing rights. This affirmative action program was challenged in court by non–First Nations fishers, including John Michael Kapp, as a violation of equality. McLachlin and Rosalie Abella wrote the main decision upholding the affirmative action program and also stating that the framework in *Law* was too complex to work well. They declared that an approach similar to that in *Andrews* was better after all. Although McLachlin had signed on to the *Law* decision nine years earlier, her decision in *Kapp* shows her willingness to admit mistakes, and move on for the sake of improving legal clarity.

The *Kapp* decision was also important for being the first Supreme Court decision to signal the Court's willingness to give teeth to the affirmative action part of section 15, the second part of the equality clause in the *Charter*. This section states that affirmative action programs — where governments seek to ameliorate the conditions of groups that have been subjected to discrimination in the past — are constitutional. The McLachlin-Abella decision upheld the right of the government to implement the affirmative action program challenged by Mr. Kapp.

During her last month writing decisions in 2018, Beverley McLachlin wrote a strongly worded dissent that illustrates her commitment to equality rights. In *Centrale des syndicats du Québec v. Quebec*, the issue was whether a six-year delay beginning in 2001 in ensuring equal pay for work of equal value in Quebec was a violation of the section 15 equality guarantee in the *Charter*.[51] The delay was caused by the time required to develop a formula for assessing equal pay for work of equal value in workplaces without male comparators, and by the time needed for government officials to negotiate a solution with employers. McLachlin and four other judges found that the delay violated section 15, but four of these judges wrote that the delay could be justified as a reasonable limit. McLachlin, however, was not convinced that the government required so much time to negotiate. The delay, she wrote, resulted in unnecessary suffering to women who were already vulnerable and disadvantaged.

McLachlin helped to clarify the framework for the Court to use in determining section 15 violations. As well, her care in analyzing complex evidence allowed her to support the equality claims of vulnerable and disadvantaged people, while deferring to governments where discrimination is not so clear.

THE IMPACT OF McLACHLIN'S DECISIONS ON CANADA

McLachlin is an unassuming, nonpartisan, nonideological person who has tried to do her best to contribute to Canadian society through her service on the Supreme Court. Because of her down-to-earth approach, it is easy to miss the importance of the impact that she has had on Canada through her decisions — whether written singly or collaboratively.

It is evident that McLachlin has put a good deal of energy, thought and analysis into her decisions. She has advanced democratic rights by extending the franchise to prisoners. She has helped advance Aboriginal rights and ensure that *Charter* rights are protected for the most vulnerable in society, including those suffering from debilitating diseases, those accused of terrorism, sex workers and those addicted to hard drugs, and prisoners. Overall, she has been a strong defender of equality. She is Canada's "reasonable person" imagined by jurisprudence.

7

Dissident in Search of Consensus

In the ceremony in the courtroom of the Supreme Court building at which McLachlin was sworn in as Canada's seventeenth chief justice on January 7, 2000, she was welcomed by senior Associate Justice Claire L'Heureux-Dubé. L'Heureux-Dubé referred to McLachlin as a "dissident in search of a consensus" — as someone who listens, who is both efficient and pleasant, but "not afraid of the heat."[1]

As an associate justice, McLachlin participated in writing seventy-eight judgments (decisions she either authored or co-authored) that either a majority or all of the other judges agreed with. As well, she wrote 115 sets of separate reasons: fifty-eight dissents and fifty-seven separate concurrences, reaching the same outcome as the majority but for different reasons.

Thus she wrote separately more often than she wrote for the majority. As L'Heureux-Dubé pointed out, she was a judge "in search of a consensus" — but not at the cost of abandoning her principles. It was not so much that McLachlin as associate justice was contrarian, but that the Court under Chief Justice Lamer was fractured. The tensions on the Court distressed and upset McLachlin,[2] but her ability to tackle them was limited until she became chief justice.

McLachlin told us that she tried very hard to develop consensus as chief justice:

> *I can't explain exactly how it happened. But the whole Court, for most of the period when I was chief justice, were of the view that we ought to minimize our differences without compromising any of our principles, and we were told that that was much appreciated by the bar and the bench.*[3]

When we asked her about her frequent separate decisions earlier in her Supreme Court career, she noted,

> *There was a period early on when I was dissenting. Part of that could be the way the Court was made up. Part of it's the issues . . . I think there's value in dissent, but I have always felt that there was value in a strong majority. Long before I was chief justice, I would often say I would put some water in my wine without compromising basic principle. But I always tried to concur when I could. But if I had a different perspective, I stated it.*[4]

In a December 2017 television interview, McLachlin was asked, "How do you feel you've changed the Court?" Her response was, "I've tried to encourage consensus, I've tried to encourage collegiality."[5]

Statistical analysis of Supreme Court decisions from 2000 to 2017 indeed demonstrates that the proportion of consensual decisions increased significantly, and that the tendency for judges in earlier courts to divide themselves into fairly consistent voting groups virtually disappeared in the McLachlin Court. McLachlin clearly did change the Court to be both more consensual and collegial, and these changes became an important backdrop to the major decisions that were made during her tenure.

BUILDING CONSENSUS

The Supreme Court keeps statistics on how many of its decisions were "unanimous as to outcome" — one of the measures that showed some improvement, albeit modest, from the Lamer Court to the McLachlin Court. The McLachlin Court was unanimous as to outcome nearly 69 per cent of the time, compared with 63 per cent for the Lamer Court.

However, this measure does not address the number of "separate concurrences" — in which justices agree on the decision's outcome, but differ on the reasons that justify that outcome. Such disagreement is important, because the reasons for the decision constitute the precedent that will constrain future and lower courts. The specific outcome — who wins and who loses — matters a great deal to the immediate parties, but it is the reasons for the outcome that matter to lawyers, judges in courts below and Canadians in general. As U.S. Supreme Court Justice Antonin Scalia famously said, a judgment that gets the reasons wrong gets everything wrong — the purpose of a judgment is to provide reasons.[6]

A more useful measure, therefore, is not how many judgments were unanimous as to outcome, but how many were "univocal"[7] as to the reasons supporting that outcome. On this measure, McLachlin's more consensual claim is even more credible. Univocal decisions accounted for 42 per cent of decisions during the Lamer Court, but for a dramatically higher 57 per cent of McLachlin Court decisions.

Even this measure, however, does not provide the full picture regarding consensus levels among the justices. We need to have some idea about the number and size of the fragments when the Court did split. Sometimes, the Court is unanimous except for a single judge (for the Lamer Court, usually L'Heureux-Dubé; for the McLachlin Court, usually Suzanne Côté). Sometimes a panel divides much more spectacularly. In *Haaretz.com*,[8] for example, there were five different sets of reasons, and in *Mikisew Cree*[9] there were four, none of which gained the signatures of more than three judges.[10] While both an 8–1 division and a 3–3–1–1–1 fragmentation represent decisions that are "not unanimous as to outcome," the latter fragmentation demonstrates far less unity. A precise way of measuring the extent of fragmentation is called the "sum of squares." This formula calculates the degree of unity among the judges, whether it is the court that presents a single decision or nine separate decisions. A score of 1 indicates complete agreement in all decisions, and a score of 0.111 would mean that each judge writes separate decisions all the time.[11]

On this more robust measure, the McLachlin Court clearly succeeded in reducing the fragmentation of its predecessor. The overall unity index score for the Lamer Court's reserved judgments was 0.730; the corresponding score for the McLachlin Court was 0.824. Not only can we say that the McLachlin Court was less divided than its predecessor, but we can say how much less divided it was. Panel fragmentation was reduced by just over one-third. This validates McLachlin's claim that hers was a more collegial court.

The point is not that perfect unity — every decision both unanimous and univocal — was ever McLachlin's target, or that such a target would be achievable, or even desirable, on a court like the Supreme Court. The cases that come before the Supreme Court involve issues that are both complex and highly important. They often raise completely new questions; not infrequently, the Court's judgment will begin by acknowledging an issue that has never before been brought before it. Dissents and separate concurrences alike can serve a useful purpose by highlighting aspects of the matter that may have been finessed by the majority, or by registering concerns about some aspect or implication of the majority reasons.

Minority reasons are much more than an empty gesture without judicial consequences. In fact, minority reasons are cited and their ideas incorporated surprisingly frequently. During the 1990s, just under one in every ten of the Supreme Court's judicial citations referred to minority reasons.[12] McLachlin's target was not to eliminate the minority reasons that divided the Court but to contain them, especially with respect to "plurality judgments" where no single set of reasons has drawn the support of a panel majority. In this endeavour, McLachlin was extremely successful.

ENCOURAGING COLLEGIALITY

McLachlin also strove for a more collegial environment among the Supreme Court justices. Greater collegiality means more participation involving a larger number of judges in the process of constructing opinions — whether majority judgments, separate concurring opinions or dissenting opinions.

The Supreme Court has for some time adopted a procedure that involves circulating draft reasons within the panel, inviting critical suggestions that will often be incorporated within the draft and then circulated again. That is to say, even a decision that is attributed to a single author in the Supreme Court Reports is to this extent a collegial product, and interviews with judges about the process make it clear that both suggestions and revisions at the early draft stage are taken very seriously. However, McLachlin's comments in the television interview seem to suggest that she did something more than simply continue the Court's decades-old practices, and we concur.

"Circulate and revise" is more collegial than pure solo authorship, but a more formal and explicit acknowledgment of shared responsibility for delivering the reasons for judgment is more collegial yet. That is precisely the practice that most clearly differentiates the McLachlin Court from its predecessor courts. A significant proportion of her Court's decisions, skewed towards the more important decisions, acknowledged two (or three, or five, or all nine) of the judges as equally sharing the writing. For a recent example of this trend, consider *"Carter 2,"*[13] which responded to a government request for extending the deadline for amending the *Criminal Code* with respect to assisted suicide. The Court split nearly down the middle. Five judges jointly wrote a majority decision approving the application, while four judges jointly wrote a dissent. To describe this outcome, "two sets of jointly authored reasons," as being unusual would be an understatement, not just in terms of the history of our Supreme Court,[14] but for the common law judicial world more generally.

The most dramatic form of co-authorship is the "By the Court" judgment — a set of reasons that is usually (but not quite always) supported by the unanimous panel but presented in a way that declines to identify a lead author or authors from among the members of the panel.[15] This practice dates back fifty years[16] and has at the time of writing accumulated about five dozen significant examples. It is really without parallel in the common law judicial world.[17] We have only been able to find a single comparable example in the United States Supreme Court,[18] and another single comparable example in the Supreme Court of the United Kingdom.[19] If the practice is fifty years old, the McLachlin Court can hardly be credited with inventing it, but it can certainly be described as having used it more often and more systematically than any of its predecessors.

The Supreme Court of Canada's "By the Court" practice tends to be used for constitutional law decisions in general, and federalism cases in particular. It is, for example, the Court's preferred way of answering a reference question from the federal government. The power of the federal government to ask the Supreme Court a direct question poses a practical problem for the Court because the reference question process is so removed from the normal appeal-court context. At one time, well into the 1960s, every judge on the Court would write their own response and reasons (a practice known as seriatim), but the "new" practice — never followed more frequently than by the McLachlin Court — has involved the anonymous and unanimous response of a "By the Court" judgment.[20] Two of the major decisions we mentioned in earlier chapters as making a lasting mark on Canadian constitutional law took this form — the *Securities Reference* and the *Senate Reference*. The *Supreme Court Reference* might also be thought of as nearly in the "By the Court" category, despite Michael Moldaver's solo dissent, because the six judges in the majority wrote a joint opinion. Linguistic analysis indicates that McLachlin was likely the lead author of both the *Senate Reference* and the *Supreme Court Reference*, and was a possible lead author of the *Securities Reference* along with Morris Fish and Rosalie Abella, but this analysis also demonstrates the significant involvement of other judges in the decision writing.[21]

Another practice that marks the McLachlin Court is the production of judgments that are attributed to two or more of the judges on the panel.[22] This practice also predates the McLachlin Court, but only slightly. In the closing years of the Lamer Court, a flurry of judgments (sixteen in its last twenty-four months) were jointly attributed to a pair of judges — but the core of that set of decisions was the unusually cooperative interaction between a single pair of judges, Peter Cory and Frank Iacobucci, one or both of whom were involved in almost all of the examples.[23]

This joint authorship of judgments not only continued, but dramatically expanded under the McLachlin Court, with more than 120 examples. Every single judge who served under McLachlin was involved in at least one co-authorship, and every single year saw multiple examples.[24] The large number of two- and three-judge groupings were heavily skewed towards the more significant decisions, and particularly towards decisions on constitutional law (the *Charter*, federalism and Indigenous issues) and public law in general.

The frequency with which a decision is cited is one measure of its importance — in that context, the four most frequently cited decisions of the McLachlin Court were all jointly authored. For the last three years of the McLachlin Court, a judge's participation on the panel for a reserved decision was more likely to result in a shared co-authorship than the solo authorship of a judgment.[25] Nor did McLachlin use co-authorship to advance her own influence. At no time during the eighteen years of her chief justiceship was McLachlin the most frequent participant in co-authoring decisions.

A review of the most cited decisions from the ten judges who retired most recently from the McLachlin Court further highlights the importance of co-authorship in the Court. For five of those ten judges (McLachlin, Louis LeBel, Louise Charron, Michel Bastarache and John Major), their most cited case involved a co-authored decision.[26]

When we spoke with her, McLachlin described co-authorships as emerging from the post-conference hearings voluntarily and more or less spontaneously, a product of the Court itself rather than of her leadership. She also presented co-authorships as a spontaneous gesture on the part of an initial solo lead author to a colleague or colleagues who provided particularly extensive and helpful responses during the "circulate and revise" process. With respect, we think this may understate her role. In a personal conversation, a former member of her court explained the rise of co-authorships in terms of the chief justice vigorously encouraging a negotiated co-authorship as a solution to what would otherwise have been an extended separate concurrence.

Some negotiated co-authorships are genuine meetings of the minds, and in this way help to clarify the law. Some, however, are unavoidably compromises, the price of which may be incompleteness or vagueness with respect to at least some of the problem points.[27]

If two or more different sets of judges tended to co-write only within their own group, this would not indicate anything particularly collegial about the court as a whole. However, our analysis shows that a consistent splinter-group tendency was clearly not the case in McLachlin's Court. One of McLachlin's most significant impacts as chief justice was to foster — whether deliberately or through her own example — the almost complete absence of such factions.

The development of small subgroups within a larger group is in itself neither sinister nor suspicious. Within a small group that interacts continuously on important matters over an extended period of time,[28] each member necessarily becomes aware of the varying values and priorities of the others, and in particular which of them tend to share, at least to some useful extent, the same values. Over time, this awareness will generate clusters of judges who tend to vote together, and that in turn may make interaction within and between the resulting clusters an important element of how the court reaches its more challenging decisions. Applied to the Canadian Supreme Court, identifying the clusters has served as a useful way to explain certain aspects of the court's decision-making.[29]

There is a methodology for teasing out the partnerships and groupings within the Court. The first step is to narrow consideration to the non-unanimous cases and determine how often each judge voted with the majority.[30] Second, within the broad set of non-unanimous cases, examine the two-judge interaction for every pair of judges to see how often they signed on together. This step will identify cooperative clusterings that could overlap to create a group like the "gang of five" in the Lamer Court. Third, find the significant decisions of the Court that are explained by the clusterings, and in particular by the relative success of the "in group" that may have emerged from the first two steps.

This methodology, applied to the Laskin, Dickson and Lamer Courts, showed consistent voting partnerships.[31] However, this analysis yielded absolutely nothing for the McLachlin Court. There has of course been a tendency for certain pairs or even trios of judges to agree more often than average on divided panels, but the differences were modest and never added up in a way that explained any of the Court's major decisions. When we mentioned this finding to McLachlin, she commented,

That's right. Well I worked very hard on that. And there's lots of ways you do that — by going around, seeing everybody. You do that by trying to have events where you include all the judges. You try to develop collegiality in different ways, and try and get everyone to see their role from an institutional perspective as well as individual, but understand and appreciate that the institution is the important thing. That's what speaks to Canadians and Canadian people — it's the Supreme Court. They are much less interested in whether my name is on the decision or somebody else's name, because they want to see what the Court decided. So, I always felt that we needed to function really well as an institution — that everybody should understand that institutional perspective.[32]

In an interview in 2015, McLachlin said she was aware that people often talked about "blocs" on the Supreme Court and tried to find them on her Court, but she found this an "amusing fiction."[33] That being the case, we must acknowledge that we were among the people who amused her.[34]

It strikes us as a remarkable accomplishment that McLachlin succeeded in preventing the development of consistent voting blocs on the Court, all the more so because of the circumstances that prevailed as she became chief justice. The personnel of the Court she inherited was initially largely unchanged from the Lamer Court of the previous decade, the Court for which the "gang of five" analysis is the most solid confirmation of group-formation theory. A reasonable expectation, therefore, was that these alliances might survive the change in chief justiceship in such a way that her previous status as one of the "outsiders" would be problematic. Instead of a chief justice who centred the dominant group, we would have had one who had been outside that group and now, at best, worked on its margins.[35]

Further, during her chief justiceship the membership of the Court swung from almost all Liberal government appointees to almost all Conservative government appointees. Even if Canadians have avoided the deep partisan rift that disfigures the United States Supreme Court, one might have expected some elements of emerging differences roughly coinciding with the government appointing the judges. But, remarkably, there is no evidence of any voting blocs, let alone those coalescing around the party of the appointing prime minister.

The co-authorships described above are both part of the explanation for this state of affairs and its logical outcome. In terms of the voting blocs that might have emerged as they did prior to McLachlin's chief justiceship, the joint authorships weaken rather than reinforce them, which suggests strategy rather than casual spontaneity. There were forty-seven different combinations involved in the multi-judge shared authorships during the McLachlin era (and even more if we were to include shared authorships of minority reasons). Whether by chance or design, the enhanced collegiality of co-authorship has developed as a practice that steadily undermined the formation of reasonably stable voting groups.

The outcomes of decisions on the McLachlin Court were demonstrably not the product of an in-group that sometimes absorbed and sometimes simply prevailed over an identifiable and predictable subset of the Court. Even its divided decisions (demonstrably less common than for predecessor Courts) revealed shifting rather than enduring alliances of in-groups and out-groups. During our interview with McLachlin, we pointed out that there were forty-four different pairs of judges and three different trios that wrote co-authored decisions on her Court. She was genuinely surprised. However, she thought that this result was "excellent."[36]

In a similar vein, the rather surprising frequency of identifiable "swing judgments" — where the judge initially assigned the writing of the judgment lost enough signatures to become the writer of minority reasons — has demonstrated a flexible willingness to be persuaded on the part of the Court's members.[37]

A further development during the McLachlin era is the decline in "named" citations by the Supreme Court. This refers to a practice related to judicial citations — a favoured device in the judicial explanation tool chest. A judicial citation is a direct reference to an earlier decision of the Court, often (a remarkably stable and persisting 40 per cent of the time) accompanied by a direct quotation from that earlier case. This citation serves to explain the immediate decision by fitting it in with previously established law, and to de-emphasize any originality or creativity in favour of a stress on continuity.

As recently as the 1990s, the convention of naming the writing judge as you quoted the decision was pervasive.[38] This of course meant a higher profile for the more frequently cited judges. Particular judges tended to be cited more frequently, with the implicit message that the words should be more persuasive because of the name to which they were attached, and because the name was referred to so often. The oft-cited names included Bora Laskin, Brian Dickson, Bertha Wilson, Antonio Lamer, Gérard La Forest and Frank Iacobucci. Earlier on, Lyman Duff, Ivan Rand and Francis Anglin were frequently cited. Naming names is how an institution tells the stories about its own history, and these are the names around which the institutional history of the Supreme Court was implicitly being organized.[39]

Over time, however, the practice of citing previous decisions with names attached has become less common. The citations continue, but the number of times names are attached has steadily declined. On the Dickson Court, cited decisions included specific names 45 per cent of the time. On the Lamer Court, it was 40 per cent. On the McLachlin Court, it started at 30 per cent and then gradually slid down to just over 20 per cent. Attributing this to McLachlin's personal leadership, or at least her example, is fully justified. On the Lamer Court, she was something of an outlier, who named a cited or quoted judge much less often than any of her colleagues, but her own Court has evolved so that during the last few years of her tenure, she was "middle of the pack" in this respect.

When we pointed out this trend to McLachlin, this was her comment:

> *I feel that if you get too much of this [in a decision], names and citations, and so on, in, you make the decision very dense and hard to read. People have to skip over a whole clump of stuff to get to the next idea. So I like to keep the narrative flowing. And where names and things interfere with that, I tend not to, just as a matter of style.*[40]

The Court's more recent style reflects a different presentation of itself, as the individual judges increasingly vanish behind more institutional labels. Citations now usually identify cited cases in terms of "the Court" having decided something, even though older judgments almost always had a solo author, and even the more recent ones usually had either a solo author or a co-writing pair. The point of the earlier "naming names" approach was that it implied the authority of the named judge. The point of the newer approach is that the name of the cited judge no longer matters.[41]

This new approach very much meshes with the new tendency to use co-authorships for a disproportionate number of the more important decisions. Even quoted citations are only half as likely to be attributed to named individuals if the judgment in question has been co-authored. Indeed, these developments represent two different sides of the same coin. Earlier decisions are less likely to be cited or quoted as the product of a specific individual, and current decisions are less likely to be delivered in the form of a decision attributed to a single judge, especially for the more important constitutional and public law decisions.

THE McLACHLIN TRANSFORMATION

Indeed, McLachlin left the Supreme Court much more consensual and collegial than it was before she began her chief justiceship. First, she has increasingly been the person on the Court who embodies its "institutional memory." Canadian practice ensures that the chief justice will always be one of the most senior members of the Court, and the steady turnover on the Court during her unusually long chief justiceship has steadily ratcheted up the importance of this factor.

Another element is her remarkable work ethic. She stayed on top of all of the judgments that were being written and circulated, identified possible points of congruence between judgments and emerging separate concurrences to encourage co-authorships, noticed unnecessarily pointed remarks so as to gently ask the author to reconsider them, and all this while providing something of a social centre for the Court and a routine mentoring process for the more junior members. Add to this the administrative and "outreach" elements of the chief justice's job, and it all adds up to a punishing workload, which from all indications she has handled gracefully.

Finally, McLachlin practised what she preached. The chief justice essentially decides who writes the judgment in any decision, so she could have assigned as many of the most important decisions to herself as she wished. Instead, the most important of the Court's judgments were parcelled out in a remarkably even-handed way. McLachlin as chief justice delivered fewer of the "top twenty" judgments for her court, and penned a lower proportion of top cases than any of her three predecessors as chief justice. The six most frequently cited decisions of her Court were written or co-written by eight different judges; the twelve most frequently cited by twelve different judges; the top twenty by seventeen different judges.[42]

There is something of a paradox here. On the one hand, the Supreme Court has gained a higher profile in recent decades, emerging as a key national institution constantly dealing with constitutional issues. Meanwhile, the dynamics of the modern news process tend to emphasize individuals over institutions — in this case Beverley McLachlin. Her profile is enhanced by her status as the first woman to serve as chief justice and reinforced by the remarkable duration of her tenure in office. On the other hand, she has worked with remarkable success to "share the load" and reduce the profile primacy of any individual within the decision-making and judgment-delivery process, which works very much in the other direction.

During the McLachlin era, we have moved beyond the age of the heroic Court with its heroic judges into the age of the institutional Court, where things are done by and attributed to the Court as a whole or shared between two or more individuals. This approach is completely consistent with the way that McLachlin talked about herself and the Court in the personal interview that she gave us. The pronoun "I" was entirely reserved for talking about her life before she was appointed to the Supreme Court. For talking about anything during her chief justiceship, personal agency was never claimed, and our every question was answered with "we" or "my colleagues" or "the Court."[43] This approach again demonstrates that for her, collegiality is not just a way of saying "we get along reasonably well and courteously" but rather "we operate as much as we can in a collective and institutional way." We see this as her major contribution to the Court, the most important way in which she has transformed the institution.

McLachlin's approach is also completely consistent with the literature on gender differences in behaviour within organizations, the "Gilligan thesis."[44] Women are more co-operative and collaborative, less competitive, less "trophy"-motivated. They are more empathetic and more concerned about others' feelings. However, what we have gleaned from McLachlin's speeches over the years is that she is a champion of women's equality not because women are different, but because they deserve the same respect and opportunity in society as men. We view McLachlin's approach as chief justice as the product of her personhood, including life lessons learned, her principles and her humanity.

McLachlin is well aware of the challenges faced by liberal democracy around the world, and she views impartial, independent and effective judiciaries as institutions that can help to address such challenges. She sees Canada as having developed innovations in jurisprudence and judicial decision-making that might serve as examples in other countries.[45] Keeping this exemplary role in mind, there are signs of an operating strategy in McLachlin's approach.

First, reduce disagreement and fragmentation within panels to get away from the "swing vote rules the Court" and the "next appointment changes everything" dynamic that has been driving commentary about the U.S. Supreme Court in recent decades. When there is disagreement, lower the tone within which that disagreement is expressed. Avoid the vitriol that stokes resentment and counter-responses (something that will forever cloud the legacy of U.S. former justice Antonin Scalia[46]). Avoid too the fiery rhetoric that stirs up a wider public,[47] in favour of a low-key civility — less exciting perhaps, but ultimately more effective. The problem is not only that the "other side" might want to get even with rhetoric of its own, but that the public is invited to view the Court's decisions as the product of angry factions that do not deliberate but simply call each other names, exhibiting a lack of respect that invites wider imitation. McLachlin's very simple tactic for containing any such tendency on her own Court was to point out through casual conversation any potentially hurtful or belittling phraseology, inviting its rephrasing in more temperate terms.[48]

Second, prevent the Court from dividing into recognizable voting blocs, with a "gang of whatever" on one side and the constant losers on the other. Such a division almost guarantees that the two blocs will be available for recruitment by major social actors in a divided and potentially polarized society, with every new appointment assessed for its impact on the balance between the two groups and its potential for a magical "fifth vote" shift. Instead, establish a Court that not only splits less often but does so on the basis of constantly shifting alliances — a Court that presents itself as transparently responsive to persuasion, not a Court of fixed voting blocs and solid positions.

Third, reduce the importance of judgments attributed to individual judges (given the broader public's under-appreciation of the extent to which the "circulate and revise" process has for decades made every judgment something of a collegial product), because of the way that solo attribution has the potential to turn individual judges into champions or villains for specific groups or interests. Especially for the more significant cases that are expected to have enduring significance, use co-authorship or even anonymous and unanimous authorship to shift the attention away from individual judges and towards the institution.

Fourth, adopt a new attribution style. McLachlin recognized that routinely attaching the names of individual judges to the outcomes of controversial cases promotes rather than contains the potential for the Court to be perceived as partisan. This tendency can be blunted twice, first by the assignment of judgments to duets or trios of judges rather than a single author who will "wear" the decision forever, and second, by framing the citation as "the Court decided."

On all four counts: create a Court that is not like the United States Supreme Court, which has been widely perceived as having been captured by the great culture wars that have transformed American politics into endless ugly conflict. Not all decisions of that Court are divided, but the major ones are — to such an extent that a book on the subject carried the revealing title *The Puzzle of Unanimity*,[49] as if the simple fact of that Court reaching general agreement on anything was in itself puzzling.

Consternation arises among American liberals whenever there is a headline about Ruth Bader Ginsburg's health, and the Senate Republicans refused even to begin token consideration of President Obama's nomination to fill the vacancy on the Supreme

Court caused by Justice Scalia's sudden death in 2016. This is not a happy corner for a national high court to find itself in. Chief Justice McLachlin was determined that the Supreme Court of Canada would not go in that direction under her watch. Her legacy as an individual judge may reside in the reasons she wrote for the Court. However, her legacy as a chief justice is demonstrated by the collegiality-creating institutional practices she established as a routine part of the Court's operations.

8

Showdown: Prime Minister vs. Chief Justice

On May 1, 2014, Prime Minister Stephen Harper issued a press release accusing Chief Justice McLachlin of improper behaviour. He claimed that she had tried to contact him in July of 2013 regarding the filling of a vacancy for one of the Quebec seats on the Supreme Court. Harper described this as an attempt at "lobbying," which would violate the constitutional buffers between the government and the judiciary.

On May 2, Harper openly criticized a decision of the McLachlin Court. Harper's statements stunned Canadians and dominated news headlines. Never before had a Canadian prime minister publicly criticized a chief justice. Politicians criticizing judges violates the constitutional convention of judicial independence. The reputations of both the chief justice and the Supreme Court were at stake, as well as the principles that protect judicial independence and the rule of law.

This episode revolves around two themes: the constitutional convention of judicial independence and the legal issue regarding qualifications for judges appointed to the Supreme Court from Quebec. We explain how both of these combined to create a crisis for both McLachlin and Harper.

JUDICIAL INDEPENDENCE

Judicial independence means that judges have the power to make decisions in cases based solely on the evidence presented to them in court, thus freeing them from interference outside the court process. The concept is designed to promote judicial impartiality. A foundational constitutional principle that has been evolving for centuries, judicial independence is essential to maintaining the rule of law.[1]

The principle rests in part on politicians refraining from criticizing judges or their decisions and judges refraining from commenting on political issues. Criticism of judges or of specific judicial decisions by politicians would constitute pressure on judges to decide as the government would prefer them to, as opposed to deciding impartially. If a government as litigant disagrees with a lower court decision, the appropriate action is to appeal. Similarly, criticism of politicians by judges would draw the judges into the political realm, eroding the appearance of impartiality and tempting politicians to respond. References to judicial independence in Canada's written Constitution are general, and we rely on convention — unwritten constitutional principles developed over time — to protect the specifics.[2]

Judicial independence has been relatively well understood and respected by Canadian judges and politicians in our modern history, but there have been occasional lapses, mostly by politicians. Between 1971 and 1976, there were two examples of cabinet ministers who contacted or tried to contact judges while the judges were considering legal issues, and both of these were considered violations of judicial independence.[3] The accepted punishment was for the cabinet minister either to apologize or resign, depending on the seriousness of the situation, although the offender could be reappointed to cabinet after an appropriate hiatus. In 1976, a minister in Prime Minister Pierre Trudeau's cabinet, André Ouellet, publicly criticized a judicial decision. Not only did he resign from cabinet, but he was also convicted of contempt of court.[4] Also in 1976, Trudeau issued guidelines to cabinet to ensure that they understood they could neither contact judges about a proceeding nor criticize judicial decisions. In spite of these guidelines, in 1978 and 1990, cabinet ministers contacted judges inappropriately, and the ministers resigned in both cases.[5]

On February 11, 2011, Jason Kenney, then a cabinet minister in the Harper government, gave a speech at the University of Western Ontario Faculty of Law in which he sharply criticized several decisions of Federal Court judges. Kenney was not required by Harper either to resign or to apologize for this clear violation of judicial independence.[6] Kenney's attack on judges with impunity marked a retreat from the standards of respect for judicial independence that had been widely observed in Canada. However, Stephen Harper's broadside on Beverley McLachlin on May 1, 2014, along with subsequent comments, was even more serious.

THE LEGAL ISSUE

The central legal issue concerned how the Canadian Constitution defines the qualifications for judges appointed to the Supreme Court from Quebec; this engages deep historic differences about the uniqueness of Quebec's legal regime. In 1763, France ceded Quebec to the British after France's military defeat on the Plains of Abraham in 1759. The British aimed at imposing their own legal system on the French-speaking inhabitants, but the first two governors, James Murray and Guy Carleton, found that the best way to rule Quebec and win the loyalty of the inhabitants was to maintain the French civil law system. The *Quebec Act of 1774* entrenched French civil law as a permanent feature of Quebec.[7]

In 1867, the Canadian Constitution granted the provinces control over private law,[8] which meant that the French civil law system continued for private law in Quebec. The main difference from English common law is that the French system involves the development of a single all-embracing statutory code rather than an evolving aggregation of freestanding statutes against a background of judicial precedent. When the Supreme Court of Canada was established in 1875, the legislation provided for one-third of the judges to be appointed from Quebec, so that when Quebec civil law appeals are heard by the Supreme Court, panels can include Quebec judges who are experts in the Quebec civil law. After 1949, when Supreme Court was enlarged to nine with three of the judges from Quebec, it became possible to form a panel of five that included a majority of Quebec judges.

The *Supreme Court Act* clarifies the "from Quebec" guarantee by identifying three groups from which the Quebec appointments can be made: the Quebec Court of Appeal, the Quebec Superior Court and members of the Quebec bar with ten years of experience. Because of the routine consultations that take place with the chief justice about Supreme Court appointments, McLachlin knew that some of those being considered by Prime Minister Harper — specifically, some Quebec members of the Federal Court of Appeal and the Federal Court — might not fit the category of "members of the Quebec bar with ten years of experience."

This raised a concern because the Federal Court is a specialized court that hears cases involving matters such as immigration, admiralty law, patents and judicial review of federal administrative decisions. Its jurisdiction does not cover Quebec civil law, thus raising the question of whether Federal Court judges from Quebec fit the criteria for Supreme Court appointments, given that they do not work in an area involving Quebec civil law. McLachlin wanted to alert Harper about this potential issue; to her, this was a legitimate part of the consultation process regarding appointments to the Supreme Court.

But the Supreme Court nomination unfolded against a larger backdrop, in particular the fact that the prime minister and his cabinet were increasingly frustrated by an extended string of high-profile case losses in the Supreme Court.[9] We therefore need to place the dispute in a wider context, that being the post-*Charter* controversy about judicial activism and judicial restraint that had been brewing throughout McLachlin's judicial career.

Harper was a fierce critic of what he considered judicial activism. Although we would not label McLachlin an activist (and we have some doubts about the utility of the label itself), she was certainly not restrained when faced with clear violations of the rule of law. The story of their clash illuminates important aspects of what it means to have a powerful court with an extensive constitutional caseload in these changing times.

JUDICIAL ACTIVISM AND RESTRAINT

The *Charter of Rights and Freedoms* became part of Canada's Constitution in 1982, a year after Beverley McLachlin was first appointed as a judge. Although the *Charter of Rights* was popular with Canadians from the start and continues to be so,[10] there was a good deal of worry among lawyers and academics in the early 1980s about how judges would interpret it. As the Supreme Court started handing down its early *Charter* judgments in the late 1980s, numerous books were written criticizing the judges, either for conceding too frequently to government arguments for narrow definitions of or reasonable limits to rights (i.e., judicial restraint), or for striking down too many laws enacted by elected legislatures (judicial activism).[11]

Those who criticized the Supreme Court for being too activist argued that in a democracy it is elected legislatures that express the "will of the people," validated by their electoral accountability, so judges should only use the *Charter* to strike down legislation in the most exceptional circumstances. During our careers, we have interviewed judges appointed both before and after the *Charter of Rights*, including Supreme Court judges. Many of the judges appointed before 1982 told us that they had not wanted to be put into a position to strike down legislation under a constitutional *Charter of Rights*, had not wanted "enforce (and explain) the law" to morph into "second guess the legislatures on rights."[12] However, having a constitutional *Charter* that would give judges the power to strike down legislation formed a key part of the national debate about the *Charter* from 1980 to 1982, and most Canadians supported the idea of giving judges this enhanced power.

Indeed, entrenching the *Charter* in 1982 brought a change to the role of judges and courts in Canada, notwithstanding the fact that judges had always used their power to strike down legislation from time to time if a federal or provincial government was overreaching its constitutional jurisdiction. Entrenchment of the *Charter* meant that a much wider range of public policy issues was brought before the courts. Many of these involved very high-profile matters that vividly captured public attention, such as gay rights, abortion, assisted suicide and prostitution.

The *Charter* had been carefully framed to recognize the ultimate power of legislatures to make the law. It is part of the supreme Canadian law and it can be amended, if necessary, through joint action of Parliament and provincial legislatures. Furthermore, governments can argue under section 1 of the *Charter* that challenged legislation should be upheld as "reasonable limits" to *Charter* rights by demonstrating that some government objectives are important enough to limit rights. In addition, some rights can be overridden by legislatures for five-year periods by invoking the "notwithstanding" clause of section 33 of the *Charter*; this is a consideration that ten years ago we would have described as something of a dead letter but that has been brought back into active consideration in recent years by provincial premiers in Ontario and Quebec.[13]

We think that in present-day Canada, the balance between legislative and judicial powers — between elected officials and appointed judges — is about right, although we acknowledge that reasonable people can reasonably disagree. However, some elected politicians of all political ideologies remain convinced that judges should be considerably more deferential to laws enacted by elected legislatures and more willing to interpret constitutional provisions in ways that give greater leeway to legislative choice or executive action. Stephen Harper was one such politician.

THE HARPER GOVERNMENT'S LOSSES IN COURT

Beginning in 2008, Stephen Harper's government lost a series of cases in the Supreme Court, and these defeats clearly irked the government.[14] We consider some of the highest-profile examples:

- In 2008 and 2010, a unanimous Supreme Court ruled in favour of Omar Khadr, emphasizing the serious violations of his *Charter* rights that had occurred. The government rejected the court's urging that Khadr be returned to Canada from the U.S. prison in Guantánamo Bay, Cuba, to be dealt with under Canadian law. The Khadr decisions dismayed the Harper government, partly because the judges who decided in favour of Khadr included those who had been appointed by Harper or his Conservative predecessor, Brian Mulroney. The Khadr cases had gone from trial in the Federal Court to the Federal Court of Appeal. In both cases, of the thirteen judges (one trial judge, three Court of Appeal judges, nine Supreme Court judges) who had taken part in the two Khadr cases on three levels of court, the only one who ruled in favour of the government was Marc Nadon, a Federal Court of Appeal judge from Quebec.[15]

- The federal government had been surprised and embarrassed by a unanimous decision in 2010 that invalidated its proposed legislation to set up a national securities regulator.[16] Regulating securities in Canada has long been a matter of provincial legislation, but the global financial crisis led to an argument that the absence of uniform rules made

national government regulation desirable. Several provinces opposed the proposals, and the assumption was that
a Supreme Court decision on a federal reference question
would strengthen Ottawa's hand in these negotiations. The
move backfired badly, with a unanimous Supreme Court
finding that the federal government did not have the jurisdiction to pass the proposed statute, urging instead that the
government observe the principles of co-operative federalism.

- The *Insite* case in 2011 brought another stinging rebuke to
  the federal government.[17] An arrangement between federal
  and provincial governments had permitted the establishment
  of a safe injection site for hard drug addicts in Vancouver that was exempted from the relevant provisions of the
  Criminal Code. Although safe injection sites are defended
  by some as the appropriate way to contain the health risks
  of drug use, others condemn them for directly encouraging
  and facilitating the use of prohibited drugs and for indirectly
  contributing to the criminal behaviour that underlies these
  activities; still others object to the impact of such facilities on the immediate neighbourhoods. When the federal
  government announced that it would not be renewing the
  arrangement, it was taken to court and ultimately told in
  a unanimous decision delivered by the chief justice that it
  had to keep the safe injection site open on *Charter* grounds.

- In December 2013, in the *Bedford* case, the Supreme Court
  struck down the *Criminal Code* provisions surrounding prostitution, provisions the government would very
  much have preferred to leave in place — again a unanimous decision, and again delivered by the chief justice.

- On April 11, 2014, in three unanimous decisions, the court
  adopted a liberal interpretation of the government's "truth in

sentencing" legislation, thus continuing to allow trial judges greater discretion in taking into account pre-trial time spent in custody than the government would have preferred.[18]

- The Supreme Court's decision in the *Senate Reference* was released on April 25, 2014, a week prior to Harper's attack on Beverly McLachlin, and it ruled out both of the government's unilateral legislated changes (advisory elections and limited-time terms for Senate appointees) as unconstitutional. This decision ended any hope that the Conservative government had of creating an elected Senate. Transforming the Senate into an elected body was a legacy of Stephen Harper's early Reform Party commitments, a long-time goal to which he devoted considerable attention and political capital in spite of the obvious constitutional hurdles. The Supreme Court decision clarified that the only way to achieve this change would be through a constitutional amendment that included support from most of the provinces. However, most provincial governments, Alberta at the time being the only exception, had no interest in making such a change. Harper was therefore obliged to announce publicly that he was giving up on his efforts to reform the Canadian Senate.

In the middle of all this, reinforcing the federal government's frustration in the most dramatic way possible, came the appointment of Marc Nadon to the Supreme Court, along with the Supreme Court reference question about Nadon's eligibility to sit on the Supreme Court, and the decision that it provoked. Supreme Court appointments do not usually result in court challenges that embarrass prime ministers and change our understanding of the Constitution, but this one did — and once again it was through an all-but-unanimous decision joined by two of Harper's own appointees. To understand this episode fully, and why it provoked the prime minister to an unprecedented public confrontation, it will be useful to examine in more detail the process leading up to Nadon's appointment and the constitutional issues that it raised.

THE NADON APPOINTMENT

In April 2013, Justice Morris Fish, one of the three Quebec judges on the Supreme Court, told McLachlin that he would retire in August, and McLachlin informed Prime Minister Harper in person so that he could initiate the process for finding a replacement.

Given the setbacks that the Harper government had experienced regarding key Supreme Court decisions, it was clear that the judges Harper had appointed prior to this time were not as deferential as he had hoped, and Fish's retirement provided an opportunity to select a judge with a record of restraint. On June 11, it was announced that a short list of six would be drawn up by the offices of the prime minister and the minister of justice.[19] The short list would be presented to a selection committee composed of three Conservative MPs (one of whom was a lawyer), one Liberal and one NDP member. The selection committee would choose three from the short list, and then the prime minister would select one of these for the Supreme Court appointment.

A search among judges from Quebec's Superior Court and Court of Appeal indicated few potential candidates with records of judicial restraint, and no experienced member of the Quebec bar stood out as an advocate of restraint.[20] The Prime Minister's Office and the Department of Justice, according to Sean Fine in *The Globe and Mail*, decided to widen the search, and identified Marc Nadon. In the end, three of those on the short list were judges then sitting on the Federal Court of Appeal, including Nadon. Another one was a Federal Court judge, and two were jurists on the Quebec Court of Appeal.[21]

Although Federal Court judges had been appointed to the Supreme Court in the past to represent a common law province, a Federal Court judge had never been appointed to fill a Quebec seat. This is because Federal Court judges do not deal with Quebec civil law issues, and the longer they sit on the Federal Court, the greater the chance that they may not be up to date on developments in civil law. This presumably explains the fact that the appointment criteria for the "three Quebec seats" identified in the *Supreme Court Act* are not quite identical to those for the other six. Former members of the provincial bar are eligible for appointment for the nine common law provinces, but not for the single civil law province.

In July, 2013, the parliamentary selection committee began to consult about the names on the short list, and Chief Justice McLachlin was consulted on July 29. After seeing the short list with four names from the Federal Court or Federal Court of Appeal, McLachlin wanted to ensure that the Prime Minister's Office was aware of the potential constitutional issue regarding the eligibility of Federal Court judges to fill Quebec seats on the Supreme Court. On July 31, McLachlin's office phoned the prime minister's principal secretary and the justice minister's office to alert them, and McLachlin herself spoke to Justice Minister Peter MacKay. Her office also made preliminary inquiries about contacting Stephen Harper either in person or by telephone to ensure that he was aware of the issue, but in the end, she decided not to.[22]

Because of the issue regarding whether Federal Court judges may be appointed to fill a Quebec seat, the Privy Council Office sought legal opinions about the matter. The PCO obtained a favourable opinion from retired Supreme Court Justice Ian Binnie. Later, Professor Peter Hogg and retired Supreme Court Justice Louise Charron also provided opinions supporting Binnie's analysis. However, at least one other constitutional expert — Peter Russell — was contacted by the PCO and expressed the view that Federal Court judges were not eligible to fill seats on the Supreme Court reserved for Quebec. Perhaps because of Russell's preliminary assessment, he was not asked to submit a formal opinion.[23]

The parliamentary selection committee, with a majority of Conservatives, had to choose three of the six candidates from which the prime minister would make a selection. Because there were four candidates from the Federal Court, at least one of them would necessarily end up on the short list of three, and as it happens, that was Nadon. On September 30, 2013, Harper announced in Parliament that his nomination to fill the vacant Quebec seat on the Supreme Court was Marc Nadon, and an ad hoc parliamentary committee subjected Nadon to questioning on October 2.[24]

On October 7, Marc Nadon was sworn in as a Supreme Court of Canada judge. On the same day, his appointment was challenged as invalid by Toronto lawyer Rocco Galati.[25] Galati was a sole practitioner in Toronto who practised immigration and national security law.[26] He sometimes represented clients in the Federal Court where Marc Nadon had been a judge.[27] Galati was familiar with the qualifications for judicial appointments to the Supreme Court in the *Supreme Court Act*, and he believed that Federal Court judges, including Nadon, were not eligible for appointment to one of the three Quebec positions. Because of the litigation, Nadon was not assigned to hear cases on the Supreme Court, including the case dealing with his appointment.

Ten days later, on October 17, the government of Quebec also initiated a legal challenge to Nadon's appointment. The Quebec government has always staunchly defended Quebec's civil law system and remained vigilant about the risk of final decisions being made by a mostly-common-law Supreme Court; the guarantee of three Quebec judges and the practice of smaller Quebec-dominated panels for civil law appeals have provided an important reassurance.

The Quebec government was not convinced that a Federal Court judge was a legally valid choice to sit on Supreme Court panels deciding Quebec civil law issues. Appeals from Quebec that involve significant issues of Quebec civil law can be heard by panels of five on the Supreme Court, and such panels can include the three judges from Quebec – which normally means the three judges with a solid experience of Quebec civil law. If one of the three Quebec judges cannot sit with one of these panels, an ad hoc judge is chosen from the Quebec Court of Appeal or the Quebec

Superior Court. A Federal Court judge is not entitled to sit ad hoc on the Supreme Court,[28] presumably because of a lack of recent familiarity with Quebec civil law.

Realizing its vulnerability on the appointment issue, the government wasted no time in preparing a counter-strategy. On October 22, the government introduced amendments to the *Supreme Court Act* as part of an omnibus budget bill. The amendments would make it possible for someone who had been a member of the Quebec bar for ten years but who was not currently a member (such as Nadon), to be eligible for appointment to the Supreme Court.[29] On the same day, the cabinet sent a reference question to the Supreme Court asking about both the eligibility issue and the constitutionality of the October 22 draft amendments to the *Supreme Court Act*.

In March 2014, in a majority decision that included the two remaining Quebec judges, the court ruled that Nadon's appointment was invalid, as were the proposed amendments to the *Supreme Court Act*.[30] The majority judgment is attributed jointly to McLachlin, LeBel, Abella, Cromwell, Karakatsanis and Wagner; Moldaver wrote a solo dissent.

The majority ruled that the *Supreme Court Act* requires that the three judges from Quebec must have a recent background in Quebec civil law, so that the five-judge panels assigned to hear Quebec civil law appeals always can have a majority of Quebec judges who are actively experts in Quebec civil law. Although Nadon had at one time practised civil law in Quebec, he had not done so during his two decades on the Federal Court, and of course his membership in Quebec's law society had ended with his first judicial appointment.

The majority opinion quoted from Peter Russell, one of Canada's leading constitutional experts, emphasizing the importance of ensuring that the Quebec judicial appointees are current in Quebec civil law. In 1969, Russell completed a study of the bilingual and bicultural aspects of the Supreme Court of Canada for the Royal Commission on Bilingualism and Biculturalism,[31] in which he emphasized the importance to Quebec's remaining in Canada of the Supreme Court's ability and credibility to hear Quebec civil law appeals:

> *The antipathy to having the Civil Code of Lower Canada [Quebec] interpreted by judges from an alien legal tradition was not based merely on a concern for legal purity or accuracy. It stemmed more often from the more fundamental premise that Quebec's civil-law system was an essential ingredient of its distinctive culture and therefore it required, as a matter of right, judicial custodians imbued with the methods of jurisprudence and social values integral to that culture. [emphasis in original.]*[32]

The decision had even wider implications because the reference question included the matter of the Harper government's proposed amendments to the *Supreme Court Act*. The Court used the opportunity to spell out the Supreme Court's constitutional status in light of certain ambiguities resulting from the 1982 constitutional amendments. In the long run, this clarification — to make the Supreme Court part of the Constitution of Canada that can only be amended with provincial consent — may well represent the enduring element of the *Supreme Court Reference*, but it was the Court's invalidation of the Nadon appointment and the resulting Harper-McLachlin confrontation that drew attention in Canada and abroad at the time.

A PRIME MINISTER ENRAGED

The Harper government's loss in the *Supreme Court Reference* case in March 2014 was followed a month later by its loss in the *Senate Reference*. At the end of April, a columnist for the *National Post* learned about the Harper government's rising anger towards the Supreme Court, and in particular towards its leader, Chief Justice Beverley McLachlin. On May 1, the paper published a story claiming,

> *Rumours [from the cabinet] about Beverley McLach-*
> *lin, the Chief Justice, are being shared with journalists,*
> *alleging she lobbied against the appointment of Marc*
> *Nadon to the court (an appointment later overturned as*
> *unconstitutional).*[33]

For Stephen Harper, the *National Post* article provided an opportunity to go public with his frustrations about McLachlin and her court.[34] Harper expressed his annoyance about McLachlin in a press release issued by the Prime Minister's Office later on May 1. The press release accused McLachlin of trying to contact Harper inappropriately about a legal issue that had or may come before the Court. It stated,

> *Neither the Prime Minister nor the Minister of Justice*
> *would ever call a sitting judge on a matter that is or may*
> *be before their court. The Chief Justice initiated the call*
> *to the Minister of Justice. After the Minister received her*
> *call he advised the Prime Minister that, given the subject*
> *she wished to raise, taking a phone call from the Chief*
> *Justice would be inadvisable and inappropriate.*[35]

If indeed McLachlin had tried to contact Harper inappropriately, reported *The Globe and Mail,*

> *The longest-serving chief justice in the court's history*
> *might have to resign, or face the unheard-of prospect*
> *that the House of Commons and Senate would unite to*
> *force her off the bench.*[36]

As it turned out, Harper's accusation was not true. McLachlin had been delivering a speech at the University of Moncton when Harper's statement was released, and she was on her way to catch a plane back to Ottawa when she heard about the prime minister's press release. She said, "I obviously was shocked and dismayed . . . I thought, 'this is not right. This is not true.'"[37]

Later that morning, McLachlin met with Owen Rees, her executive legal officer, and told him, "We're going to put out a statement and deny any wrongdoing — which there was none — and just set out the facts."[38] Her May 2 press release read in part as follows:

At no time was there any communication between Chief Justice McLachlin and the government regarding any case before the courts. The facts are as follows:

On April 22, 2013, as a courtesy, the Chief Justice met with the Prime Minister to give him Justice Fish's retirement letter. As is customary, they briefly discussed the needs of the Supreme Court of Canada.

On July 29, 2013, as part of the usual process the Chief Justice met with the Parliamentary committee regarding the appointment of Justice Fish's successor. She provided the committee with her views on the needs of the Supreme Court.

On July 31, 2013, the Chief Justice's office called the Minister of Justice's office and the Prime Minister's Chief of Staff, Mr. Novak, to flag a potential issue regarding the eligibility of a judge of the federal courts to fill a Quebec seat on the Supreme Court. Later that day, the Chief Justice spoke with the Minister of Justice, Mr. MacKay, to flag the potential issue. The Chief Justice's office also made preliminary inquiries to set up a call or meeting with the Prime Minister, but ultimately the Chief Justice decided not to pursue a call or meeting.

The Chief Justice had no other contact with the government on this issue.

The Chief Justice provided the following statement: "Given the potential impact on the Court, I wished to ensure that the government was aware of the eligibility issue. At no time did I express any opinion as to the merits of the eligibility issue. It is customary for Chief Justices to be consulted during the appointment process and there is nothing inappropriate in raising a potential issue affecting a future appointment."[39]

The contacts McLachlin had had with the prime minister and his office, Justice Minister Peter MacKay and the parliamentary search committee that ultimately recommended Nadon's appointment all constituted part of the normal but very limited types of communication that exist between a chief justice and the government regarding the retirement of judges and appointment of their replacements. These communications are necessary because of the federal cabinet's constitutional duty to appoint judges and the responsibility that the minister of justice and parliamentary search committees have to consult the chief justice about potential appointments. If undertaken appropriately, these in no way violate the constitutional principle of judicial independence. Chief Justice Brian Dickson and Prime Minister Mulroney "established a regular practice of consultation for Supreme Court appointments,"[40] and Chief Justice Lamer remarked that he was "always" consulted about appointments.[41]

Later on May 2, Stephen Harper made additional remarks at a press conference that clearly violated the principle of judicial independence. According to a Canadian Press report, Harper said that were the prime minister or other minister of the Crown to consult a high court judge about a case due to come before the courts,

I think all the opposition, the media and the legal community would be completely shocked by that kind of behaviour.

What I did was appropriate: I consulted both internal and external constitutional experts, and I allowed the Supreme Court to make its own decision.

Harper also said the decision to reject Nadon means that Federal Court judges from Quebec are essentially ineligible to sit on the high court, a circumstance he said he considers unfair.

Through this decision, the reality is that the Supreme Court has decided that a Quebec judge at the Federal Court is a second-class judge.

All the other judges from all the other provinces have the possibility of a promotion to the Supreme Court, but not Quebec judges — they no longer have that right, as others do.

Harper's statement was factually wrong. When McLachlin alerted the minister of justice on July 31, 2013, about the eligibility issue, there was no case "due to come before the courts." As McLachlin herself noted, she was merely trying to flag the eligibility issue, and she had no opinion one way or another on it at that time. Moreover, it was McLachlin who decided in the end not to set up a call with the prime minister; it was misleading for Harper to state that he had refused the call.

Worse, Harper went on to severely criticize the Supreme Court decision about Nadon's eligibility and to claim that the decision had turned Quebec judges on the Federal Court into "second-class" judges. At this point, following constitutional convention, Harper should have either apologized or resigned. He did neither. Constitutional conventions are enforced by the electorate, not by the courts, and Harper's inappropriate statements may have been a factor that led to his government's defeat in the 2015 election.

The Canadian legal community reacted quickly to protest the prime minister's accusations about McLachlin and his lack of respect for judicial independence. More than 650 lawyers signed and published a statement supporting McLachlin, including eleven past presidents of the Canadian Bar Association and the Council of Canadian Law Deans.[42] Former Progressive Conservative Prime Ministers Joe Clark and Brian Mulroney backed McLachlin, as well as former Liberal Prime Ministers Jean Chrétien and Paul Martin.[43] An investigation by the International Commission of Jurists in Geneva condemned Harper's breach of the norms of judicial independence.[44] McLachlin refrained from criticizing the prime minister, and simply set out the facts dispassionately. She carried on as chief justice for three and a half more years until her retirement.[45]

The fact that a prime minister so blatantly violated the constitutional convention of judicial independence indicated that he either disagreed with the principle or did not understand it. Constitutional conventions are designed to promote democratic accountability; their value lies in their ability to evolve over time, both to improve and to adjust to societal changes. Their weakness is that political leaders and ordinary citizens may not understand the conventions or may take advantage of insufficient public knowledge about them.

In response to this challenge and in reaction to abuses of power by some politicians, in 1979 the New Zealand Cabinet Office wrote down the British constitutional conventions as they then applied to New Zealand in a guidance document called the Cabinet Manual.[46] The 2017 edition of this document states,

> *Ministers must exercise judgement before commenting on judicial decisions, whether generally, or in relation to the specifics of an individual case . . . [and] should not*

express any views that are likely to be publicised if they could be regarded as reflecting adversely on the impartiality, personal views, or ability of any judge.[47]

Given Harper's missteps, we think Canadian federal and provincial cabinets should consider following New Zealand's example.

McLachlin's calm but firm handling of the dispute with Prime Minister Harper in 2014, and her fierce defence of the Supreme Court's reputation and of judicial independence generally, make up an important part of her enduring legacy.

Footprints in the Sand? Or Handprints in Cement?

I've always been fascinated by those issues that really divide society.

The big issues — we've been able to resolve them in a peaceful way, even where our population is very divided, by saying that we'll all have a say in the process, and ultimately the Court will come up with a decision.

Maybe if the government doesn't like [the Court's resolution], they will change it a bit. But we have a process, a process that by and large has served us well. And I'm just hoping that we can continue that process for the big issues for the future. Because if we don't get that right, it's going to be very difficult for a very diverse, multicultural society to move forward together.

— Beverley McLachlin, interview with the authors,
April 9, 2018

Beverley McLachlin's legacy may well be determined by whether the decision-making process that she helped to refine during her twenty-eight years on the Supreme Court of Canada, and especially during her seventeen years as chief justice, continues to "serve us well."

McLachlin has always felt up to the challenge of tackling difficult issues. Her talent stems from a natural inclination, nurtured by her family experience and tempered by having to be tough and resourceful during her teenage years living on a ranch in the foothills of the Rocky Mountains. She was never one to accept an ordinary way forward in life when extraordinary opportunities presented themselves. Her hard work in high school resulted in scholarships that enabled her to attend university in Edmonton. She fell in love with philosophy and thus learned methodologies for resolving complex issues. She enjoyed the challenge of practising law in Edmonton, Fort St. John and then Vancouver, and in particular the complexities of high-stakes litigation. She began what would have been a distinguished academic career, but decided it would be wise to accept the judgeship offered to her in 1981, at the same time honouring her responsibilities as a mother and spouse.

From her law school days through to her lawyering through to her university teaching and research, McLachlin was recognized for being bright, competent, well organized and detail-oriented, but also collegial and unassuming. She could be counted on to do what she said she would do and to do it thoroughly, insightfully and honestly.

On the basis of the values that McLachlin learned from her upbringing, she has always felt a duty to try to make the world a better place — to contribute to resolving the issues that "really divide society." As a judge, her tools were the rule of law, conscious objectivity (reasonableness, humanity and compassion to fill in legal gaps) and a thorough review of evidence. The hard issues that she tackled in her decision-making included dying with dignity, Aboriginal land claims, the rights of prisoners and those detained for national security reasons, hate speech and prostitution. Her decisions, and those made with her colleagues on the Court, contributed to lowering the temperature on the secession debate and to determining the future course of the Senate and the Supreme Court itself.

Her promotion of collegiality and consensus on the Supreme Court presented an even greater contribution. Through example and encouragement, she invited her fellow judges to consider more carefully ideas to which they might initially be averse and to find a way to work effectively with each of their colleagues. The result was a Court that spoke more clearly and convincingly than perhaps ever before. We know that McLachlin's style of deliberation on the Court was not always welcomed by all of her fellow judges. Some would have preferred more in-person conferences[1] and free-for-all discussions, while McLachlin favoured careful individual analysis and exchange of ideas through Court memos. Her approach resulted in a more unified, less friction-prone Court.

McLachlin is remarkable for her long service as a judge — thirty-six years from her appointment to the County Court in B.C. in 1981 to her retirement in 2017. Before becoming a judge, and while she was a professor of law at the University of British Columbia, she started to write a novel, something she had wanted to do since her high school days in Pincher Creek. With retirement looming in 2017, she dusted off the old manuscript and brought it up to date, and it hit the book stores a few months after she retired. The result is a page-turner thriller about a young woman lawyer who defends those with seemingly hopeless cases.

This first novel gave McLachlin a chance to tell a story in a way that she couldn't as a judge. It not only allowed her to fulfill a life-long ambition, but it was the first of many retirement projects. In addition to working on other writing projects, McLachlin sits on the Singapore International Commercial Court[2] and on the Court of Final Appeal in Hong Kong.[3] She believes that Canada has much to offer the rest of the world from its jurisprudence and advances in our legal system — she worked tirelessly as an advocate of access to justice as president of the Canadian Judicial Council — and she wants to take opportunities to help resolve "issues that really divide us" internationally.

Given that in recent years it has become the norm for Supreme Court judges to retire prior to the compulsory retirement age of seventy-five, we asked McLachlin if she had ever considered retiring early. She responded,

> *No, no. For me, I loved the Court, and I could not think of a better thing to do. I could not think of a more satisfying, honourable, wonderful place to be. And I was able to deal with it. I mean every personality is different, but I dealt with it in a way that was not affecting my health negatively, and it kept stimulating me, and so it was a good place for me to be.*[4]

Her response indicates that she had not only a love of law and her work on the Supreme Court, but good coping skills, which surely originated in Pincher Creek. In a small community, one encounters many different personalities, and must learn how to get along with them all. Small town life is in this respect quite different from that of the big cities in which so many Canadians now live. We think this is relevant because an appeal court like the Supreme Court of Canada is the ultimate small community, a small group with a leisurely turnover rate and with intense and frequent interaction between all of its members. The patterns that emerge from this can involve in-groups and out-groups (like the "gang of five'), or solitary mavericks on the fringes[5] or personal differences that fester for years or even decades.[6] The level of collegiality is unusual not only in terms of the history of the Supreme Court of Canada itself, but also by comparison with other similar courts. The fact that disagreement rates on the Court started to rise again in 2018[7] shows how difficult it is to maintain such an interactive partnership; harder still was the careful patience required to establish it in the first place.

A number of McLachlin's previous colleagues did choose to retire prior to age seventy-five. We asked McLachlin about the tendency of Supreme Court judges since the mid-1970s to retire early. From 1947 to 1973, all but one of the judges appointed to the Supreme Court[8] served to age seventy-four or seventy-five, even when the term was twenty-four or twenty-five years long. Suddenly, in 1973, this practice stopped.[9] Now the normal service has dropped to an average of ten years. McLachlin responded to this observation as follows:

> *That was the expectation [when I became a judge], that you would serve out your life, or at least until your retirement. My own view . . . it's a multifactored thing. I think the work on the Court is much more demanding, and it really requires a great deal of continued, sustained effort, and it's wearing. A lot of people say, "I can do it for ten years, and then I have to do something else." And so, after the pension laws changed . . . and they said a Supreme Court justice could leave with full pension after ten years — that's a big factor . . . So [new judicial appointees] sometimes came here thinking that they would do ten years, and then go off and do something else. And another factor is that people are living longer, and they are seeing that there is another life for them after the Court, and if they want to get on with that life, they'd better do it sooner rather than later, establish yourself, because the later it is, the harder it is in theory, they think anyway, so people leave. So, I think it's a combination of changed pension and retirement laws, the difficulty of the work. Since the eighties and nineties when the Charter came in, and the heavy load, and the fact that people are living longer and they are viewing*

retirement differently — they are seeing something after retirement.[10]

In the mid-1990s, we interviewed judges on the Supreme Court of Canada as part of a project on appellate court decision-making in Canada. We mentioned to McLachlin that when we interviewed Supreme Court judges at the time, most seemed tired and stressed, with three exceptions — John Sopinka, Claire L'Heureux-Dubé and her. Her response was,

> *When I came to the Court in 1989, they were tired . . .*
> *They were just inundated, not only by huge numbers of*
> *cases, but they had to figure things out in a way that no*
> *other Court had ever had to do. What is this document*
> *— the* Charter *— going to mean? And by and large they*
> *did an incredible job . . . They could have gone other*
> *ways, and maybe that would have been all right too, but*
> *what they did has proved to be worthy. And they laid*
> *out a pretty good foundation in those early years. But it*
> *was enormous work, and they were tired. And there were*
> *costs to their health. And you were seeing that in [your*
> *interviews].*[11]

Our observation during our mid-1990s interviews was that the judges who did not seem tired and stressed had found a good work-life balance. We asked McLachlin about her work-life balance strategy:

> *Yes, well that's very important. I replaced Justice [Wil-*
> *liam] McIntyre on the Supreme Court. I asked him, if*
> *you have one piece of advice to give me, what would it*
> *be? And he thought about it, and he said, "Have some*
> *outside interests, because otherwise this job will consume*
> *you." I think that's a danger — you get consumed by*

the job to the point where you don't have outside ways
of destressing. And, you know, problems — does this
person agree with me, or not — seem bigger than they
really are. And so, as a way of keeping perspective, I've
always had outside interests. It has really been a saving
thing for me.[12]

One of McLachlin's outside interests has been visiting art gal-
leries, ever since her days as arts editor of the student newspaper
at the University of Alberta. She also enjoys opera and symphony
concerts. Another interest has been playing the piano — she took
piano lessons in Ottawa to improve her technique until she became
chief justice. When her teacher said she wasn't practising enough,
she gave up the lessons, with the hope of restarting them when she
retired.[13]

Finally, we asked McLachlin how she would define the challenges the Supreme Court would face in the future:

A challenge for any institution these days is keeping
up with the rapid change that is going on in the world,
including digitalization of everything. It's changing
things for how we think about the rule of law . . . I'm
struck by the absence of coherent frameworks as to how
we're going to handle the problem of Facebook and
privacy, and those related concerns, and ensuring that
elections and democratic processes don't get distorted.

[Commentators] say we have to regulate, but they
don't say what kind of regulations. They don't say how
they are going to enforce these regulations. I think the
rule of law [in general] . . . is going to face a lot of chal-
lenges in maintaining itself. We've always had a system
where when rights conflict, people have differences,
governments and citizens have differences, governments
and governments. They come to court, and the court

resolves it, and we move on. But some of these problems that we're facing now are not actually getting into the court, and I'm not sure they're capable of that mechanism. So, the question is, how are we going to resolve those conflicts? What are we going to do about them? I think it's really going to be a challenge to the rule of law — legislators, obviously, but also judges.

And a lot of cases may not even come to courts the way they did before. How are you going to get things like whether data were used to undermine the last election into court? It's already happened and you've moved on, and the world's moved on, before you ever understand what really happened. Everything is so complex and so fast, and it's moving at such an exponential rate. I'm not saying we can't do it, but I think we need to [find a way to do it] if we really prize the rule of law and the society that we've built based on rule of law. Where all power is exercised in accordance with the rule of law, we are going to have to do some hard work, and it's going to require a lot of buy-in from people. I just don't know how it's all going to happen, but I'm hoping it will.[14]

Throughout this book, we emphasized McLachlin's faithfulness to the rule of law as one of the hallmarks of her jurisprudence. Thanks to her background in philosophy and law, her master's thesis and her four decades as a judge, she is passionate about the capacity of the rule of law, properly applied, to settle deep disputes by applying reason over impulse and facts over falsehoods. It is no wonder that she is so cognizant of the contemporary threats to the rule of law.

In addition to the increasingly sophisticated ability of social media to break the law with impunity, in 2018 we witnessed the governments of Canada's two most populous provinces declare their willingness to invoke the "notwithstanding" clause to override

Charter of Rights protections for poorly articulated reasons.[15] As well, if courts are to be as useful as they were in the past, they need to be enabled to resolve pressing issues significantly more quickly. The digital revolution, if skilfully applied, may help to speed things up, but big changes in procedure will be required, both from the legal profession and from the courts.

Not only has McLachlin had the courage to confront the "issues that really divide society," but she has developed techniques for considering these issues dispassionately, effectively and consensually. She stared down a prime minister who had no patience with a proper rule-of-law approach. Nevertheless, she realizes that, in the future, good leaders in all fields will be needed to step up and tackle new and perplexing challenges. They will determine whether her legacy turns out to be footprints in the sand or handprints in cement.

We will leave the last word to McLachlin:

> *I feel sometimes that people in my generation are not as concerned as they might be, because it's not going to be same old, same old. So [young people with an interest in tackling these issues] will be there to save us.*[16]

Acknowledgements

First and foremost, we would like to thank Beverley McLachlin for the interview that she gave us on April 9, 2018. By then, we had done much of the background research for the book, and she was able to enlighten us about the context of some of our findings.

There are many others for whom we would like to express our gratitude. Diana Reed was a close friend of Beverley McLachlin during her high school years. Reed provided us with a video recording of the speeches at the gala dinner in Vancouver in January of 2000 that was organized by friends and colleagues of Beverley McLachlin to celebrate her appointment as chief justice of Canada. There were speakers from each era of McLachlin's life up to then, and Reed spoke about the Pincher Creek years. Other speakers included Chief Justice Allan McEachern, Dennis Mitchell, James Taylor, Jim Matkin and Wilfred (Bae) Wallace. Dick Hardy, who attended high school with McLachlin, provided us with valuable insights. Farley Wuth, curator of the Kootenay Brown Pioneer Village in Pincher Creek provided us with access to the archives of the *Pincher Creek Echo*, and gave us many valuable tips. We found the investigative reporting by Sean Fine of *The Globe and Mail* useful, as well as additional materials that he shared with us.

Professor Jamie Cameron of Osgoode Hall Law School, who took a class from Beverley McLachlin when attending law school at the University of British Columbia, was kind enough both to provide us with an interview, and to review a draft manuscript. We are grateful for her insights. Our mentor, Peter Russell, also reviewed the manuscript, and made helpful suggestions.

Ian's spouse, Eilonwy Morgan, reviewed a draft of the manuscript and made numerous detailed and helpful suggestions. Ian's adult children, Christina, Philip and Girum, all contributed in useful ways.

We very much appreciate Jim Lorimer for suggesting this project to us. We are also grateful to the entire editorial and production crew at James Lorimer & Company for their patience, insight and hard work to bring this book to fruition.

Having acknowledged some of the many people who helped and supported us with this project, we also want to stress that we alone are responsible for any shortcomings herein.

Notes

INTRODUCTION

1. Beverley McLachlin, remarks on the occasion of the gala dinner to celebrate her appointment as chief justice of Canada, Vancouver, January 2000, transcribed from a video recording of the event.

2. The rule of law refers to the foundational constitutional and legal principle that the law applies equally to everyone (unless there is a valid reason in a democratic setting for exceptions), and that arbitrary decisions of government officials are unacceptable.

3. Interview with Beverley McLachlin by Peter McCormick and Ian Greene, April 9, 2018.

4. See Jamie Cameron, "McLachlin's Law: In All Its Complex Majesty," *Supreme Court Law Review* 88 (2019): 307–341, https://digitalcommons.osgoode.yorku.ca/cgi/viewcontent. cgi?article=1371&context=sclr.

5. Interview with Beverley McLachlin by Peter McCormick and Ian Greene, April 9, 2018.

6. Beverley McLachlin, "How I Became a Thriller Writer," *The Globe and Mail*, April 26, 2018, https://www.theglobeandmail.com/arts/ books/article-how-beverley-mclachlin-former-chief-justice-of-canada-became-a/. Also published as Beverley McLachlin, "And Then Fate Intervened," *The Globe and Mail*, April 28, 2018, p.18.

7. Beverley McLachlin, *Full Disclosure* (Toronto: Simon & Schuster, 2018).

8. Beverley McLachlin, "How I Became a Thriller Writer".

9. This six-month period expired on June 15, 2018.

10. Of course, the majority of decisions that she penned were of a less sensational nature, like clarifying the legal significance of the small print in insurance contracts. She never considered these cases mundane, as they relate to the rules we are all affected by on a day-to-day basis.

11. See Peter McCormick's books *The End of the Charter Revolution* (Toronto: University of Toronto Press, 2015), *Supreme at Last: The Evolution of the Supreme Court of Canada* (Toronto: Lormier, 2000) and *Canada's Courts* (Toronto: Lorimer, 1994); and Ian Greene's books *The Charter of Rights and Freedoms: 30+ Years of*

Decisions That Shape Canadian Life (Toronto: Lorimer, 2014) and *The Courts* (Vancouver: University of British Columbia Press, 2006). Together we have written *Judges and Judging: Inside the Canadian Judicial System* (Toronto: Lorimer, 1990). See also Ian Greene, Carl Baar, Peter McCormick, George Szablowski and Martin Thomas, *Final Appeal: Decision-making in Canadian Courts of Appeal* (Toronto: Lorimer, 1998).

CHAPTER 1

1. *Pincher Creek* by Robert McInnis. McLachlin first saw this painting in Antonio Lamer's office when he was an associate justice. McLachlin was impressed by it and wanted to buy it, but it is Government of Canada property, on loan to the Supreme Court. Lamer liked the painting, and it followed him to his new office when he became chief justice in 1990. It stayed in the chief justice's office when McLachlin moved into it in 2000. Sean Fine, "How Beverley Mclachlin Found Her Bliss," *The Globe and Mail*, January 13, 2018, A12, at A13, https://www.theglobeandmail. com/news/national/beverley-mclachlin-profile/article37588525/.
2. "Ernest Gietz Funeral on August 3rd," *Pincher Creek Echo*, August 10, 1977.
3. "Obituary, Otto Gietz," McInnis and Holloway Funeral Homes, December 2006, http://www.mhfh.com/gietz-otto/. Otto Gietz was a brother of Ernest. Also see Fine, "How Beverley McLachlin."
4. Fine, "How Beverley McLachlin."
5. Interview with McLachlin, April 9, 2018.
6. Cathy Lowne, "Heidi," *Encyclopaedia Britannica*, https://www. britannica.com/topic/Heidi-by-Spyri.
7   Interview with Diana Reed by Peter McCormick and Ian Greene, September 7, 2017. We first contacted Diana Reed to request an interview on August 10, 2017. However, Diana, who is about the same age as Beverley McLachlin, was helping to operate a combine, and so we arranged the interview after combining was completed in September.
8. Interview with McLachlin, April 9, 2018.
9. Alberta, "Municipal Population List," https://open.alberta.ca/ publications/2368-7320.
10. These are observations from the authors' experiences in small-town Alberta schools in that era.

11. Amy von Heyking, "Fostering a Provincial Identity: Two Eras in Alberta Schooling," *Canadian Journal of Education* 29, no. 4 (2006): 1127–56.

12. See, for example, "Pincher Creek Hutterite Colony," http://gameo. org/index.php?title=Pincher_Creek_Hutterite_Colony_(Pincher_ Creek,_Alberta,_Canada).

13. See "Piikani," *Canadian Encyclopedia*, http://www. thecanadianencyclopedia.ca/en/article/piikuni-peigan-pikuni/, and "Kainai (Blood)," *Canadian Encyclopedia*, https://www. thecanadianencyclopedia.ca/en/article/blood-kainai.

14. Fine, "How Beverley McLachlin," A13.

15. Katherine Ashenburg, "Canada's Top Judge: Chief Justice Beverley McLachlin's Remarkable Service," *Alberta Views*, September 2016, 35, at 36.

16. See Ian Greene, *The Charter of Rights and Freedoms: 30+ Years of Decisions that Shape Canadian Life* (Toronto: Lorimer, 2014), Chapter 8, "Aboriginal Rights."

17. *Alberta v. Hutterian Brethren of Wilson Colony*, 2009 SCC 37, [2009] 2 SCR 567.

18. According to the obituary of Ernest Gietz, he "served for a number of years on the clergy of the Christian church" ("Ernest Gietz Funeral," *Pincher Creek Echo*). His funeral was held at the Pincher Creek Pentecostal Tabernacle in 1977, the same church where Eleanora's funeral was held in 1972.

19. Fine, "How Beverley McLachlin."

20. Ashenburg, "Canada's Top Judge," 36.

21. Diana Reed, remarks at the gala dinner to celebrate McLachlin's appointment as chief justice of Canada, Vancouver, January 2000. Transcribed from a video recording of the event.

22. Ibid.

23. Interview with McLachlin, April 9, 2018.

24. Ibid. The old log house was destroyed by new owners after the Gietz family sold the property.

25. Fine, "How Beverley McLachlin."

26. Interview with McLachlin, April 9, 2018. Ian Greene also completed an English course by correspondence in Alberta, and attributes his early interest in writing to the quality of that course.

27. Interview with McLachlin, April 9, 2018.

28. Ibid.

29. Fine, "How Beverley McLachlin," and interview with Reed, September 7, 2017.

30. Interview with Reed, September 7, 2017.

31. Beverley McLachlin, "And Then Fate Intervened," *The Globe and Mail*, April 28, 2018, 18.

32. Fine, "How Beverley McLachlin."

33. Ibid.

34. Interview with McLachlin, April 9, 2018.

35. Ibid.

36. McLachlin, "And Then Fate Intervened."

37. Ibid.

38. Peter Feniak, "Profile Beverley McLachlin: From the Supreme Court to the Bestseller List," *Good Times*, September 2018, 10, at 12.

39. There were up to eighteen girls, and perhaps a dozen boys.

40. Reed, remarks at gala dinner, 2000.

41. Ibid.

42. Yale D. Belanger and P. Whitney Lackenbaur, Eds., *Blockades or Breakthroughs?: Aboriginal Peoples Confront the Canadian State* (Montreal: McGill-Queen's University Press, 2014).

43. Feniak, "Profile Beverley McLachlin," 13.

44. According to Diana Reed, *Messiah* was performed during their grade ten year (interview with Reed, September 7, 2017).

45. Ashenburg, "Canada's Top Judge," 36.

46. Interview with Reed, September 7, 2017.

47. "Award Presentations to Former Students," *Pincher Creek Echo*, September 21, 1961, 1.

48. Ibid.

49. Interviews with friends of Beverley McLachlin in the Pincher Creek area, August 10 and September 7, 2017.

50. Ibid.

51. Pincher Creek produced two chief justices in addition to McLachlin and Winkler. "William Ives, a cowhand as a child — who did not attend elementary school till he was 21 — was chief justice of the Alberta Supreme Court from 1942–44. Val Milvain was chief justice of the Alberta Supreme Court Trial Division from 1971–79" (Fine, "How Beverley McLachlin").

52. Interview with Reed, September 7, 2017.

CHAPTER 2

1. The average January temperature in Edmonton is 6 degrees Celsius colder than Pincher Creek. In January 1969, the daytime high temperature in Edmonton never rose above -21 degrees for twenty-six straight days.

2. "Edmonton Population History," https://www.edmonton.ca/ city_government/facts_figures/population-history.aspx. Calgary's population in 1961 was 250,000, and in 1971 it was 403,000.

3. The auditoriums were built to celebrate the fiftieth-anniversary jubilee of the province of Alberta, which was created in 1905.

4. Jim Matkin, remarks at gala dinner in honour of Beverley McLachlin's appointment as chief justice of Canada, Vancouver, 2000. Transcribed from a video recording of the event. Matkin was a classmate of Beverley McLachlin's in law school. He went on to a stellar career in law, serving as a deputy minister, and also as the secretary (a position he held at the time of the event) and executive director of the Law Society of British Columbia.

5. Rod Macleod, *All True Things: A History of the University of Alberta* (Edmonton: University of Alberta Press, 2008), 155 ff. In 1960, the University of Alberta established a satellite campus in Calgary, which became the autonomous University of Calgary in 1966.

6. Ibid., 234. The proportion of Edmonton students grew to 65 per cent in 1970 because of the growth of the University of Calgary, the University of Lethbridge and community colleges.

7. Macleod, *All True Things*, 185. In 1957–1958, six of eighty-nine law students were women.

8. "Award Presentations to Former Students."

9. "Chief Justice McLachlin Speaks About the Importance of Philosophy," University of Alberta, Department of Philosophy, September 7, 2017, https://www.ualberta.ca/philosophy/ news/2017/september/chief-justice-mclachlin-speaks-about-the-importance-of-philosophy.

10. Ashenburg, "Canada's Top Judge," 36.

11. "Chief Justice McLachlin Speaks."

12. Ibid.

13. University of Alberta, Department of Philosophy, "About the Department," https://www.ualberta.ca/philosophy/about-the-department.

14. Anthony Mardiros and William Irvine, *The Life of a Prairie Radical* (Toronto: Lorimer, 1979).

15. Interview with McLachlin, April 9, 2018.

16. Kirk Makin, "Beverley McLachlin," *Canadian Encyclopedia*, January 29, 2008, https://www.thecanadianencyclopedia.ca/en/article/beverley-mclachlin.

17. Sheelagh Matthews, "From Pincher Creek to the Supreme Court: Chief Justice Beverley McLachlin's Story," *Lethbridge Living*, Summer 2000, 20, at 21.

18. Interview with McLachlin, April 9, 2018.

19. Interviews with friends of Beverley McLachlin in Pincher Creek, September 2017.

20. Matkin, remarks at gala dinner, 2000.

21. Ibid.

22. Ivan L. Head and Pierre Trudeau, *The Canadian Way: Shaping Canada's Foreign Policy 1968–1984* (Toronto: McClelland & Stewart, 1995).

23. Matkin, remarks at gala dinner, 2000.

24. Ibid.

25. Ibid.

26. Dr. Leonard Gietz graduated fourth in his class, and went on to an accomplished career as a pathologist. See "Obituary, Leonard Geitz, M.D.," *Victoria Advocate*, April 21, 2017, https://www.victoriaadvocate.com/obituaries/leonard-paul-gietz-m-d/article_e060c635-dc1d-5401-9af8-46de4941708b.html.

27. Interview with Garth Turcott by Ian Greene, August 10, 2017.

28. Interview with McLachlin, April 9, 2018.

29. H.L.A. Hart, *The Concept of Law* (Oxford, U.K.: Oxford University Press, 1961).

30. Lon L. Fuller, "Positivism and Fidelity to Law — A Reply to Professor Hart," *Harvard Law Review* 71 (1958), 630.

31. John Austin, *The Province of Jurisprudence Determined*, ed. H.L.A. Hart (Oxford, U.K.: Oxford University Press, 1954).

32. Beverley McLachlin, "The Role of Rules in the Concept of Law"(master's thesis, University of Alberta, 1968), 127–28.

33. Ibid., 96.

34. In 1990, this firm became Weir Bowen LLP. See Philip Slayton, *Mighty Judgment: How the Supreme Court of Canada Runs Your Life* (Toronto: Allen Lane Canada, 2011, ebook location 2444).

35.   Matkin, remarks at gala dinner, 2000.

36.   Dennis Mitchell, QC, remarks at gala dinner in honour of
      Beverley McLachlin's appointment as chief justice of Canada,
      2000. Transcribed from a video recording of the event.

37.   Fine, "How Beverley McLachlin," quoting from a talk that
      McLachlin gave at the Allard School of Law History Project at the
      University of British Columbia in 2017.

38.   Nemetz was appointed to the B.C. Supreme Court in 1963, and
      became chief justice of that court in 1973. He was chief justice of
      the Court of Appeal from 1979 to 1988.

39.   Mitchell, remarks at gala dinner, 2000.

40.   Ibid.

41.   Bae Wallace, remarks at gala dinner in honour of Beverley
      McLachlin's appointment as chief justice of Canada in 2000.
      Transcribed from a video recording of the event.

42.   Interview with McLachlin, April 9, 2018.

43.   Wallace, remarks at gala dinner, 2000.

44.   Ibid.

45.   Ibid.

46.   Ibid.

47.   Interview with McLachlin, April 9, 2018.

48.   Eric Damer and Herbert Rosengarten, *UBC: The First 100 Years*
      (Vancouver: University of British Columbia, 2009), 227.

49.   W. Wesley Pue, *A History of British Columbia Legal Education*,
      University of British Columbia Legal History Papers, WP 2000-1
      (March 2000): 212, http://ssrn.com/abstract=897084.

50.   Damer and Rosengarten, *UBC*.

51.   This manuscript was eventually published as Beverley M.
      McLachlin and James P. Taylor, *British Columbia Practice*
      (Vancouver: Butterworths, 1979).

52.   Interview with Professor Jamie Cameron by Ian Greene,
      November 15, 2018.

53.   Ibid.

54.   "Ernest Gietz Funeral," *Pincher Creek Echo*.

55.   McLachlin and Taylor, *British Columbia Practice*.

56.   Beverley M. McLachlin and Wilfred J. Wallace, *The Canadian
      Law of Architecture and Engineering* (Toronto and Vancouver:
      Butterworths, 1987).

57.   James Taylor, remarks at gala dinner in honour of Beverley

McLachlin's appointment as chief justice of Canada in 2000. Transcribed from a video recording of the event.

58. Ibid.

59. Interview with McLachlin, April 9, 2018.

60. Allan McEachern, remarks at gala dinner in honour of Beverley McLachlin's appointment as chief justice of Canada in 2000. Transcribed from a video recording of the event.

61. Interview with McLachlin, April 9, 2018.

62. Ibid.

63. Ibid.

64. Ibid.

65. Remarks of Allan McEachern.

66. Ibid.

67. Wallace, remarks at gala dinner, 2000.

68. Fine, "How Beverley McLachlin," 12. According to Fine, shortly after Rory's death, Beverley McLachlin went ahead with a scheduled speech: "Life was not going to overtake her."

69. *Andrews v. Law Society of British Columbia*, 1986 CanLII 1287 (BC CA).

70. Ibid., para. 33 ff. The law society appealed to the Supreme Court of Canada and lost.

71. *Andrews v. Law Society of British Columbia*, [1989] 1 SCR 143, on appeal from [1986] 4 WWR 242.

72. *Dixon v. B.C. (A.G.)*, [1989] 4 WWR 393.

73. *Reference re Provincial Electoral Boundaries (Sask.)*, [1991] 2 SCR 158.

74. Ashenburg, "Canada's Top Judge."

75. McEachern, remarks at gala dinner, 2000, and Fine, "How Beverley McLachlin," A12.

76. McLachlin got the appointment call from Brian Mulroney when she and her son Angus were visiting Australia. Angus advised her to take the job, even though she and Angus would have to move to Ottawa. Beverley's sister Judy took care of Angus in Vancouver for the rest of the school year. See Fine, "How Beverley McLachlin," A12.

77. Up to 1940, eight of thirty-six judges appointed to the Supreme Court were under forty-six years of age when appointed. Robert Taschereau, appointed in 1940, was the last of these relatively young appointees. From the time of McLachlin's appointment to

the time of writing, no judge has been appointed under the age
of fifty. From 1875, the average age of Supreme Court of Canada
judges at appointment is fifty-six.

CHAPTER 3

1.   During her time as associate justice, McLachlin was joined by
      Louise Arbour (1999–2004). After McLachlin became chief
      justice, five more women were appointed to the court: Marie
      Deschamps (2002–2012), Rosalie Abella (2004–present), Louise
      Charron (2004–2011), Andromache Karakatsanis (2011–present)
      and Suzanne Côté (2014–present). Four days after McLachlin
      retired in December 2017, Sheilah Martin was appointed.
2.   The official name for an associate justice is "puisne judge".
3.   If one or more of the three Quebec judges on the Supreme Court
      is not available to hear a Quebec civil law appeal, the chief justice
      appoints a judge of the Quebec Court of Appeal or the Quebec
      Superior Court to sit ad hoc on the Supreme Court for the appeal
      (*Supreme Court Act* [RSC, 1985, c. S-26], s. 302.)
4.   If the provincial or territorial court of appeal is divided about
      a serious criminal matter, or if the appeal court and trial court
      differ over such matters, there is a right to appeal to the Supreme
      Court. For other matters, litigants who have lost their cases in an
      appellate court must apply to the Supreme Court for permission
      to appeal. See Greene et al., *Final Appeal*, Chapter 6.
5.   The case was *R. v. Boudreau*, 2018 SCC 58.
6.   The case was *British Columbia v. Henfrey Samson Belair Ltd.*,
      [1989] 2 SCR 24, decided on July 13, 1989. This was a relatively
      straightforward case about collection of provincial sales tax from
      a bankrupt company in B.C., an issue McLachlin would have been
      familiar with from her work as a judge in the superior courts of
      B.C.
7   The case was *MacKeigan v. Hickman* [1989] 2 SCR 796.
8.   It is tempting to think of dissents as embodying "real"
      disagreement, with separate concurrences conveying something
      rather less consequential, but this assumption is premature. See,
      e.g., Peter McCormick, "Standing Apart: Separate Concurrence
      and the Supreme Court of Canada, 1984–2006," *McGill Law
      Journal* 32 (2009): 137.
9.   See, e.g., Peter McCormick, "Birds of a Feather: Alliances and

Influences on the Lamer Court 1991-7" *Osgoode Hall Law Journal* 36 (1998): 339.

10.   See, e.g., Marie-Clare Belleau, Rebecca Johnson and Valerie Bouchard, "Faces of Judicial Anger: Answering the Call," in Myriam Jézéquel and Nicolas Kasirer, eds., *Les sept péchés capitaux et le droit privé* (Montreal; Les editions Thémis, 2007).

11.   All accounts of the judgment assignment process emphasize the importance of seniority; "wait your turn" therefore has a double implication, the first involving some notional equality-approaching rotation but the second implying the need to accumulate a fairly considerable seniority before such a rotation might apply. See, e.g., Peter McCormick, "Who Writes? Gender and Judgment Assignment on the Supreme Court of Canada," *Osgoode Hall Law Journal* 51 (2014): 595.

12.   See Elliot E. Slotnick, "Who Speaks for the Court? Majority Opinion Assignment from Taft to Burger," *American Journal of Political Science* 23 (1979): 60.

13.   See Peter McCormick, "Second Thoughts: Supreme Court Citation of Dissents and Separate Concurrences, 1949–1999," *Canadian Bar Review* 81 (2002): 369.

14.   The supremacy of God may be interpreted as the recognition of freedom of conscience. See Ian Greene, *The Charter of Rights and Freedoms: 30+ Years of Decisions that Shape Canadian Life* (Toronto: Lorimer, 2014), 100–101.

15.   *Reference re Secession of Quebec*, [1998] 2 SCR 217, para. 70.

16.   Ibid., para 71. Positive law consists of legislation properly enacted, and regulations authorized by the legislation.

17.   Joseph Brean, "'Conscious Objectivity': That's How the Chief Justice Defines the Top Court's Role. Harper Might Beg to Differ," *National Post*, May 23, 2015, https://nationalpost.com/news/conscious-objectivity-thats-how-the-chief-justice-defines-the-top-courts-role-harper-might-beg-to-differ. See also Jamie Cameron, "McLachlin's Law: In All its Complex Majesty."

18.   Slayton, *Mighty Judgment*, location 1654. The retired judge spoke anonymously. See also locations 1543 and 3472 ff.

19.   See Constance Backhouse, *Claire L'Heureux-Dubé: A Life* (Vancouver: University of British Columbia Press / Osgoode Society, 2017).

20.   Ibid.

21. *MacKeigan v. Hickman.*

22. McLachlin's appointment was on March 30, 1989. The hearing in *MacKeigan v. Hickman* was on April 19 and 20. The judges present at the hearing in order of seniority were Lamer, Wilson, La Forest, L'Heureux-Dubé, Cory and Gonthier (both appointed on February 1, 1989) and McLachlin. (Neither Dickson nor Sopinka participated in the hearing.) The judges at the April 20 hearing met afterwards to discuss the outcome and decide who would write the first draft of the reasons. What is clear from the wording of the five sets of reasons is that McLachlin was initially assigned the writing of the judgment, and the writers of the other four opinions responded to McLachlin's opinion using the "I have read the reasons" protocol that acknowledge this. The Court's decision was released on October 5.

23. The constitutional issue was the scope of the principle of judicial independence, which is protected both by the *Charter of Rights and Freedoms*, s. 11(d), and by constitutional convention and tradition.

24. Chief Justice T. Alexander Hickman, Associate Chief Justice Lawrence A. Poitras and the Honourable Mr. Gregory T. Evans, *Royal Commission on the Donald Marshall, Jr., Prosecution Digest of Findings and Recommendations* (Halifax: Province of Nova Scotia, 1989), https://novascotia.ca/just/marshall_inquiry/_docs/RoyalCommissionontheDonaldMarshallJrProsecution_findings.pdf. Hickman was chief justice of Newfoundland, Poitras was from Quebec and Evans was the retired chief justice of the High Court of Ontario.

25. See Peter McCormick, "New Questions about an Old Concept: The Supreme Court of Canada's Judicial Independence," *Canadian Journal of Political Science* 37, no. 4 (December 2004): 839–62. The Hickman decision has been cited by the Supreme Court more than twenty times, including in seven cases dealing with judicial independence.

26. *Reference re Provincial Electoral Boundaries (Sask.),* [1991] 2 SCR 158.

27. *Dixon v. B.C. (A.G.),* [1989] 4 WWR 393.

28. Ian D. Izard, "The Charter and Electoral Law in British Columbia," *Canadian Parliamentary Review* 23 (Winter 1989–1990).

29.   A greater deviation from average was allowed for the two sparsely populated northern Saskatchewan ridings. No one challenged the need for greater deviation in these districts because of their geographical size.

30.   *Reference re Prov. Electoral Boundaries (Sask.)*, 34.

31.   See Ian Greene and David P. Shugarman, *Honest Politics Now: What Ethical Conduct Means in Cnaadian Public Life* (Toronto: Lorimer, 2017), 16.

32.   According to Philip Slayton, Chief Justice Lamer played very little part in writing the decision because of health challenges at the time. Iacobucci suggested that each of the other eight judges should draft one section: "Gonthier wrote the core of the judgment, and formulated the four principles." Also see Backhouse, *Claire L'Heureux-Dubé*, Chapter 34.

33.   Interview with McLachlin, April 9, 2018.

34.   Hauser Global Law School Program, New York Univesity School of Law, Distinguished Fellow Lecture Series, "To Be a Chief Justice: A Conversation with Chief Justice Beverley McLachlin," March 3, 2003. See also Slayton, *Mighty Judgment*, location 1538, and Backhouse, *Claire L'Heureux-Dubé*, 454.

35.   *Reference re Secession of Quebec*, [1998] 2 SCR 217, para. 49.

36.   Ibid., para. 54.

37.   Ibid., para. 58.

38.   Ibid., para. 63, quoting from *Reference re Provincial Electoral Boundaries* (Sask.), [1991] 2 SCR 158, at p. 186.

39.   Ibid., para. 64. Having grown up in the culturally diverse environment of Pincher Creek, McLachlin would have been cognizant of the importance of the recognition of cultural diversity in democracy.

40.   Ibid., para 68.

41.   Ibid.

42.   Ibid., para. 76.

43.   Ibid., para. 79–82.

44.   *R. v. Keegstra*, [1990] 3 SCR 197, dissenting reason of McLachlin, p. 169.

45.   Philip Rosen, "Hate Speech," Depository Services Program, Government of Canada, http://dsp-psd.pwgsc.gc.ca/Collection-R/LoPBdP/CIR/856-e.htm.

46.   *R. v. Keegstra*, [1990] 3 SCR 197.

47. Even though McLachlin advocated action against hate speech through human rights commissions instead of criminal law, she was not willing to give human rights commissions an overbroad mandate to restrict communications. She wrote a dissent in *Canada (Human Rights Commission) v. Taylor*, [1990] 3 SCR 892, a decision released the same day as the *Keegstra* decision. In *Taylor*, the majority upheld a section of the *Canadian Human Rights Act* that gives the Canadian Human Rights Commission the ability to supress messages of hatred or contempt. See also *Saskatchewan (Human Rights Commission) v. Whatcott*, 2013 SCC 1. In this decision written by Rothstein for The Court, the constitutional ability of the Saskatchewan Human Rights Commission to limit distribution of hate speech was upheld with certain restrictions.

48. *R. v. Zundel*, [1992] 2 SCR 731.

49. See Greene, *Charter of Rights*, 144 ff.

50. *Ross v. New Brunswick School District No. 15*, [1996] 1 SCR 825. La Forest dissented with McLachlin in both *Keegstra* and *Taylor*.

51. *R. v. Seaboyer; R. v. Gayme*, [1991] 2 SCR 577.

52. The other six judges who formed part of the majority were Chief Justice Lamer, La Forest, Sopinka, Cory, William Stevenson and Iacobucci.

53. See Backhouse, *Claire L'Heureux-Dubé*, 379 ff.

54. Martha Shaffer, "*Seaboyer v. R.*: A Case Comment," *Canadian Journal of Women and the Law* 5 (1992), 202, https://ssrn.com/abstract=1185581.

55. *R. v. Darrrach*, [2000] 2 SCR 443. The opinion of the Court, all nine judges participating, was written by Justice Gonthier. See Greene, *Charter of Rights*, 237–43.

56. *Rodriguez v. British Columbia (Attorney General)*,[1993] 3 SCR 519. We were told by several Supreme Court judges in the mid-1990s that the *Rodriguez* decision was the most difficult one they had ever had to make.

57. Ibid., para. 198.

58. Interview with McLachlin, April 9, 2018.

59. *Andrews v. Law Society of British Columbia*, [1989] 1 SCR 143, on appeal from [1986] 4 WWR 242.

60. Ibid., para. 34.

61. *Symes v. Canada*, [1993] 4 SCR 695.

62. *Thibadeau v. Canada*, [1995] 2 SCR 627.

63. *Egan v. Canada*, [1995] 2 SCR 513; *Vriend v. Alberta*, [1998] 1 SCR 493.

64. *Law v. Canada (Minister of Employment and Immigration)*, [1999] 1 SCR 497.

65. Cameron, "McLachlin's Law."

66. Joseph Brean, "'Reconciliation' with First Nations, Not the *Charter of Rights & Freedoms*, Will Define the Supreme Court in Coming Years,' Chief Justice Says," *National Post*, March 13, 2014, https://nationalpost.com/news/canada/reconciliation-with-first-nations-not-the-charter-of-rights-freedoms-will-define-the-supreme-court-in-coming-years-chief-justice-says.

67. *Calder v. Attorney General of British Columbia*, [1973] SCR 313.

68. See Greene, *Charter of Rights*, Chapter 8, "Aboriginal Rights: Outside the Charter but Inside the Rights Regime," 353 ff. Most scholars prefer "Aboriginal" and "Indigenous" to be capitalized when writing about section 35 issues. It is ironic that section 35 itself uses lower case.

69. *R. v. Sparrow,* [1990] 1 SCR 1075.

70. *R. v. Van der Peet,* [1996] 2 SCR 507.

71. Both McLachlin and L'Heureux-Dubé dissented from the seven-judge majority decision, but for different reasons. L'Heureux-Dubé would have sent the case back to trial for re-consideration given the guidelines provided by the Supreme Court.

72. *Delgamuukw. v. British Columbia*, [1997] 3 SCR 1010. See Greene, *Charter of Rights*, 365 ff.

73. See "Nisga'a Land Treaty," *The Canadian Encyclopedia*, retrieved from https://www.thecanadianencyclopedia.ca/en/article/nisgaa-land-treaty.

74. The panel that issued the decision was composed of six judges. La Forest and L'Heureux-Dubé wrote a separate concurring decision, and McLachlin indicated that she was in "substantial agreement" with it. This might indicated that McLachlin would have preferred a unanimous decision for clarity.

75. See Nisga'a Land Treaty, "*The Canadian Encylopedia*," https://www.thecanadianencyclopedia.ca/en/article/nisgaa-land-treaty, and Nisga'a Lisims Government, "*Understanding the Treaty,*" https://www.nisgaanation.ca/understandingtreaty.

76. *R. v. Marshall*, [1999] 3 SCR 456. See Greene, *Charter of Rights*, 370 ff.

77.   Marshall was willing to bring the case to court because of the extensive experience he had had with the justice system.

78.   *Marshall*, para. 59, p. 502 ff. The seven-judge panel consisted of Lamer, L'Heureux-Dubé, Gonthier, Cory, McLachlin, Iacobucci and Binnie.

79.   Ibid., para 68, p. 506 ff.

80.   "Maritime Waters Calm a Decade After Marshall Decision," *CBC News*, September 17, 2009, https://www.cbc.ca/news/canada/new-brunswick/maritime-waters-calm-a-decade-after-marshall-decision-1.792338.

81.   *R. v. Marshall*, [1999] 3 SCR 533. There were six judges participating in the November 17 decision, all of whom participated in the September 17 decision except for Cory, who had retired.

82.   Justice Gonthier, who concurred with McLachlin's dissent, was appointed to the Supreme Court only two months prior to McLachlin.

83.   "Maritime Waters Calm."

84.   Ian Greene et al.,

85.   Lamer retired early because of poor health and fatigue. See Slayton, *Mighty Judgment*, loc. 1544 and 3975.

86.   Ibid., loc. 3470–3478.

CHAPTER 4

1.   Sir Charles Fitzpatrick, appointed in 1906, was the youngest at fifty-two, and Antonio Lamer (CJ 1990–2000) was the second youngest at fifty-six. These three aside, the average age of a new Canadian chief justice was sixty-six.

2.   Sir William Johnstone Ritchie, who served as chief justice for thirteen and a half years in the nineteenth century, had long held this distinction; only two other chief justices (Fitzpatrick 1906–1918, Laskin 1973–1984) have served for more than ten years.

3.   This number was initially five, expanded to six in 1927 and then to the current eight in 1949.

4.   Puisne (pronounced "puny") — from the French for "born later" — refers to a judge of lesser rank than the chief judge of any court, but in ordinary usage the word has evolved to mean "weak" or "inferior" and we tend now to speak of the chief justice and the associate justices of the Supreme Court.

5.   If the *Supreme Court Act* had designated the chief justice as one
      of the nine, there might be different routes to the chief justice
      designation. Perhaps the members could designate their own
      chief, or rotate the responsibility on a limited-term basis. For a
      consideration of some of these possible alternative procedures,
      see Peter McCormick, "Selecting the Supremes: The Appointment
      of Judges to the Supreme Court of Canada," *Journal of Appellate
      Practice and Process* 7 (2005): 1.

6.   Fitzpatrick was Canada's minister of justice at the time of his
      appointment — something that would very much raise eyebrows
      today, but does not seem to have been controversial at the time.

7.   We cannot really say "terms" because in neither Canada nor the
      United States nor other comparable countries do chief justices
      serve terms of any definite length; becoming a chief justice is a
      separate appointment under the same conditions as the earlier
      appointment as an associate justice, ending with voluntary or
      mandatory retirement that takes the judge in question off the
      court altogether.

8.   Ritchie's thirteen-year tenure as chief justice of Canada in the
      nineteenth century still places him second among Canadian chief
      justices, but he is below the midpoint of the American list.

9.   This kind of scenario is far from hypothetical: after 1963, three
      chief justices (Robert Taschereau, J.R. Cartwright and Gérald
      Fauteux) rotated through the office in a single decade. That is to
      say, a judge appointed in early 1963 and retiring in 1974 would
      have served under no fewer than five different chief justices.
      No actual judge fits this description, but two come very close.
      Had Wishart Spence been appointed six months earlier, or had
      Emmett Hall retired ten months later, either of them would
      have done so. By contrast, U.S. Supreme Court Justice John Paul
      Stevens recently wrote a book entitled *Five Chiefs* referring to the
      five chief justices he had interacted with, but the account covers
      his entire career from Supreme Court law clerk in 1947 to the end
      of his thirty-five-year service on the Court in 2010.

10.   There is a strong argument that it would reinforce that
      independence more transparently and decisively if there was only
      one tradition at play, not two competing traditions that might
      sometimes create a degree of prime ministerial discretion. See
      Peter McCormick, "Choosing the Chief: Alternation, Duality

and Beyond," *Osgoode Hall Law Journal* 47 (2013): 5; and "How Should Justin Trudeau Choose the Next Chief Justice of the Supreme Court?" *Policy Options*, November 25, 2015.

11.   A tie vote — an equal number of judges supporting the "allow appeal" and "dismiss appeal" options — can still happen should one member of the panel that heard the oral arguments be unable to participate in the decision when it is handed down; the result is that the appeal fails on equal division, and the lower court decision stands. There was only a single example of equal division on the McLachlin Court, that being *R. v. L.F.W.*, 2000 SCC 6.

12.   In 2017, the Court heard sixty-nine cases, seventeen of which were as-of-right appeals. From 2007 to 2017, the Court decided an average of about seventy cases a year, and about fifteen of these annually were as-of-right appeals. See Supreme Court of Canada, *Statistics Report 2017*, https://www.scc-csc.ca/case-dossier/stat/index-eng.aspx.

13.   Andrew Heard, "The Charter in the Supreme Court of Canada: The Importance of Which Judges Hear an Appeal," *Canadian Journal of Political Science* 24 (1991): 289.

14.   For example, there was a three-month delay in the appointment of Thomas Cromwell to replace Gérard La Forest in 2008.

15.   The distinction between the judgment (the decision and reasons of the Court) and the reasons of dissenting or separately concurring minority judges is an important development dating from the late 1960s. The earlier practice was for many different judges to write reasons, for all such reasons to be considered as "judgments" and for little if any presumptively greater importance to attach to a specific set of reasons just because it had gathered more signatures.

16.   See Greene et al., *Final Appeal*.

17.   Supreme Court of Canada, *Report on Plans and Priorities (RPP) 2016–17*, https://www.scc-csc.ca/about-apropos/rep-rap/rpp/2016-2017/report-rapport-eng.aspx#s1.1.

18.   This power has recently been challenged over the proceedings on complaints about the conduct of Justice Michel Girouard of the Quebec Superior Court, at least to the extent of bringing such council recommendations within the power of judicial review through the Federal Court. See *Girouard v Canada (Attorney-General)*, [2018] FC 865.

19.   The council recommended the removal of Justice Paul Cosgrove
       in 2009 and of Justice Robin Camp in 2017. After four other
       inquiries, the council did not recommend removal, and in two
       other cases, the judge being investigated resigned or retired
       before the investigation could be completed. In 2016, the council
       initiated an inquiry into Justice Michel Girouard, but its report
       was not issued until after McLachlin retired. As president of the
       Canadian Judicial Council, the chief justice is key to organizing
       the council's proceedings, but does not participate in council
       decisions about judicial discipline. See Canadian Judicial Council,
       Judicial Conduct, https://www.cjc-ccm.gc.ca/english/conduct_
       en.asp?selMenu=conduct_judicial_conduct_en.asp.

20.   This means that McLachlin presided over the decision but did not
       vote, which makes it a little unfair that she was the target of much
       of the controversy and complaint that ensued.

21.   David Ricardo Williams, *Duff: A Life in the Law* (Vancouver:
       University of British Columbia Press, 1984), 74.

22.   Retired Supreme Court Justice Frank Iacobucci told us that one
       of McLachlin's outstanding contributions as Chief Justice was the
       superb way in which she represented and explained the court,
       both nationally and internationally. Interview by Ian Greene with
       Justice Frank Iacobucci, June 24, 2019.

23.   University of Ottawa, Faculty of Law, and Canadian Institute for
       the Administration of Justice, "Reflecting on the Legacy of Chief
       Justice McLachlin," April 10–11, 2018, https://ciaj-icaj.ca/en/
       upcoming-programs/legacy-chief-justice/.

24.   Both of these appointments are part-time.

25.   Interview with McLachlin, April 9, 2018.

26.   Greene et al., *Final Appeal*, Chapter 6.

27.   Interview with McLachlin, April 9, 2018.

28.   Comments of this kind were specifically mentioned by many
       judges whom we interviewed in the 1980s and 1990s. See
       McCormick and Greene, *Judges and Judging*, and Greene et al.,
       Final Appeal.

29.   Laskin wrote relatively frequent minority decisions with Wishart
       Spence and Brian Dickson, so that they became known as the
       "L-S-D connection."

CHAPTER 5

1.   This arrangement can occasionally be problematic: Dickson's
        biographers describe some of the difficulties he had with tardy
        responses from recently retired judges. See Robert Sharpe and
        Kent Roach, *Brian Dickson: A Judge's Journey* (Toronto: Osgoode
        Society/University of Toronto Press, 2003). More often it involves
        full and meaningful contributions. For example, one of the more
        frequently cited decisions of the McLachlin Court (*R. v. Proulx*,
        2000 SCC 5) was delivered by already-retired former Chief Justice
        Lamer.

2.   During the six month period up to June 15, 2018, McLachlin
        took part in the delivery of twenty-four decisions, writing (or
        co-writing) the judgment in four of them and minority reasons in
        five others.

3.   During the first six months of McLachlin's term, Lamer continued
        to participate in the writing of decisions for panels that he had
        sat on. His decisions were referred to as those of the "Chief
        Justice." For six months after McLachlin retired, she continued to
        participate in writing decisions for the panels she had participated
        in prior to retirement, and her decisions were referred to as those
        of the "Chief Justice."

4.   R. I. Cheffins, "The Supreme Court of Canada: The Quiet Court
        in an Unquiet Country," *Osgoode Hall Law Journal* 4 (1966).

5.   *Carter v. Canada (Attorney General)*, 2015 SCC 5.

6.   *Rodriguez v. British Columbia (Attorney General)*, [1993] 3 SCR
        519.

7   The Court does not often explicitly repudiate an earlier decision
        in such a dramatic fashion; in this context, it is worth noting that
        at the time of the *Carter* decision, McLachlin herself, who had
        dissented in 1993, was the only member of that Court who still
        serving.

8.   *Carter v. Canada (Attorney General)*, 2016 SCC 4.

9.   *Canada (Attorney General) v. PHS Community Services Society*,
        2011 SCC 44.

10.   *Canada (Attorney General) v. Bedford*, 2013 SCC 72.

11.   *Canada v. PHS*.

12.   The broader question — if the s. 7 rights of Vancouver users were
        infringed by not renewing Insite's exemption from the application
        of criminal law, what about the rights of users in places that did

not have safe injection sites? — did not come up at all.

13. *Canada (Attorney General) v. Bedford*, 2013 SCC 72.

14. *Reference re ss. 193 and 195.1(1)c of the Criminal Code*, [1990] 1 SCR 1123.

15. *Reference Re Public Service Employee Relations Act (Alberta)*, [1987] 1 SCR 313; *PSAC v. Canada*, [1987] 1 SCR 424; *RWDSU v. Saskatchewan*, [1987] 1 SCR 460.

16. *Lavigne v. Ontario Public Service Employees Union*, [1991] 2 SCR 211. The Rand system allows unions to collect dues from all members of a bargaining unit, whether or not they belong to the union.

17. *Dunmore v. Ontario (Attorney General)*, 2001 SCC 94.

18. Ibid.

19. *Health Service and Support-Facilities Subsector Bargaining Assn. v. British Columbia*, 2007 SCC 27.

20. Justice Marie Deschamps dissented in part.

21. 68 U.N.T.S. 17 ("Convention No. 87").

22. *Health Services and Support Facilities Subsector Bargaining Assn. v. British Columbia*, 2007 SCC 27, para. 81.

23. Ibid., para. 82–86.

24. *Ontario (Attorney General) v. Fraser*, 2011 SCC 20.

25. *Saskatchewan Federation of Labour v. Saskatchewan*, 2015 SCC 4.

26. *R. v. Oakes*, [1986] 1 SCR 103. A reasonable limit is one that is sufficiently important to justify limiting a right, and the objective of the limit must be rationally connected to the means used by the limit. The limit must be as little as necessary to achieve the objective, and overall a limit to a right must do more good than harm.

27. *R. v. Big M Drug Mart Ltd.*, [1985] 1 SCR 295.

28. *Syndicat Northcrest v. Amselem*, 2004 SCC 47.

29. In *Hutterian Brethren*, 2009 SCC 37 it was conceded that although religious freedom is an individual freedom, it is not without "profoundly communitarian" dimensions, which may open the door to a larger role for orthodoxy.

30. *Multani v. Commission scolaire Marguerite-Bourgeoys*, 2006 SCC 6.

31. A kirpan is a small replica of a sword that symbolizes the responsibility to cut through untruth and defend the vulnerable.

32. *Hutterian Brethren of Wilson Colony*, 2009 SCC 37.

33. *R. v. N.S.*, 2012 SCC 72.

34. *Trinity Western University v. British Columbia College of Teachers*, [2001] SCR 31.

35. *Law Society of British Columbia v. Trinity Western University*, 2018 SCC 32; *Trinity Western University v. Law Society of Upper Canada*, 2018 SCC 33.

36. But "as if" rather than literally: unconstitutional statutes or parts of statutes remain in place (we cannot say "in effect") until the relevant legislature chooses to repeal or amend them, which can take a very considerable time.

37. *Schachter v. Canada*, [1992] 2 SCR 679. See Greene, *Charter of Rights*, 288 ff.

38. For example, school busing and prison funding manded by the U.S. Supreme Court.

39. *Doucet-Boudreau v. Nova Scotia (Minister of Education)*, 2003 SCC 62.

40. Older readers will remember the years when a standard form of protest against public officials was to embarrass them by throwing (or, better yet, simply pushing in their face) a pie-plate loaded with whipped cream or shaving cream.

41. *Vancouver (City) v. Ward*, 2010 SCC 27.

42. *Gosselin v. Quebec (Attorney General)*, 2002 SCC 84.

43. McLachlin and three of her colleagues dissented in *Carter 2* on the issue of the exemption on the grounds that the complexity of instituting an exemption made this option less desirable than waiting for the government's legislative remedy.

44. In the specific case in which the Court had suggested in its statement of the constitutional issues that it would be analyzed in a focused way — *R. v. Latimer*, 2001 SCC 1 — it simply ignored the question in the actual decision.

45. An innovative remedy for unnecessary delay in criminal cases devised by the McLachlin Court in 2016 was to set a presumptive limit on the time from the filing of a case to its disposition at trial: thirty months for cases in provincial superior courts, and eighteen months for courts below that level. The majority on the court concluded that the framework developed by the Supreme Court in 1992 for determining unnecessary delay was not working. McLachlin, however, joined a separate opinion written by Cromwell that concurred in the outcome of the appeal, but

rejected the idea of rigid time limits, which could do more harm than good. Cromwell wrote that a standard of reasonableness must be applied on a case-by-case basis. *R. v. Jordan*, 2016 SCC 27, [2016] 1 SCR 631.

46. Joseph Brean, "'Reconciliation' with First Nations, Not the Charter of Rights and Freedoms, Will Define the Supreme Court in Coming Years, Chief Justice Says," *National Post*, March 13, 2014 (speech to audience of law students).

47. Beatrice Britneff, "McLachlin Cites Indigenous Rights as Source of Pride on Her Last Day at Supreme Court," *iPolitics*, December 15, 2017, iPolitics.ca; Bill Curry, "Chief Justice Beverley McLachlin Takes Pride in Work on Indigenous Rights as She Retires," *The Globe and Mail*, December 15, 2017.

48. Makin, "Beverley McLachlin," *Canadian Encyclopedia*.

49. *Guerin v. The Queen*, [1984] 2 SCR 335.

50. *R. v. Sparrow*, [1990] 1 SCR 1075.

51. *R. v. Van der Peet*, [1996] 2 SCR 507; *R. v. N.T.C. Smokehouse Ltd.*, [1996] 2 SCR 672; *R. v. Gladstone*, [1996] 2 SCR 723.

52. *Delgamuukw v. British Columbia*, [1997] 3 SCR 1010.

53. *R. v. Marshall*, [1999] 3 SCR 456.

54. *R. v. Marshall*, [1999] 3 SCR 533.

55. More precisely: *Haida Nation* was part of a trilogy: *Haida Nation v. British Columbia (Minister of Forests)*, 2004 SCC 73; *Taku River Tlingit First Nation v. British Columbia (Project Assessment Director)*, 2004 SCC 74; and *Mikisew Cree First Nation v. Canada (Minister of Canadian Heritage)*, 2005 SCC 69.

56. On the other hand, it is less restrictive than "fiduciary" because it concedes that the Crown is obliged to pursue a variety of interests, some potentially opposed to those of the specific Aboriginal community, such that balancing and proportionality considerations apply. See Ryan Beaton, *The Crown Fiduciary Duty at the Supreme Court of Canada, Canada in International Law at 150 and Beyond*, Paper No. 6 (Waterloo, ON: Centre for International Governance Innovation, January 2018), https://www.cigionline.org/sites/default/files/documents/ReflectionsSeriesPaperno.6Beaton_0.pdf.

57. See Chris W. Sanderson, Keith B. Bergner and Michelle S. Jones, "The Crown's Duty to Consult Aboriginal Peoples: Towards an Understanding of the Source, Purpose and Limits of the Duty," *Alberta Law Review* 49 (2012).

58.   *Rio Tinto Alcan v. Carrier Sekani Tribal Council,* 2010 SCC 43.
59.   *Beckman v. Little Salmon/Carmacks First Nation,* 2010 SCC 53.
60.   *Clyde River (Hamlet) v. Petroleum Geo-Services Inc.,* 2017 SCC 40.
61.   *Chippewas of the Thames First Nation v. Enbridge Pipelines Inc.,* 2017 SCC 41.
62.   *Tsilhqot'in Nation v. British Columbia,* 2014 SCC 114.
63.   *Daniels v. Canada (Indian Affairs and Northern Development),* 2016 SCC 12.
64.   The parallel question regarding whether the Inuit are included within the parameters of s. 92.14 was answered affirmatively eighty years ago, in *Reference as to whether "Indians" in s.91(24) of the B.N.A. Act includes Eskimo inhabitants in the Province of Quebec,* [1939] SCR 104.
65.   *Daniels v. Canada,* para. 53 and 56.
66.   *Manitoba Metis Federation Inc. v. Canada (Attorney General),* 2013 SCC 14, [2013] 1 SCR 623
67.   Peter Oliver has delightfully characterized this term as "a nautical analogy of dubious utility." Peter C. Oliver, "The Busy Harbours of Canadian Federalism: The Division of Powers and Its Doctrines in the McLachlin Court," in David A. Wright and Adam Dodek, eds., *Public Law at the McLachlin Court: The First Decade* (Toronto: Irwin Law, 2011).
68.   For example, the "double aspect" doctrine allows a court to characterize a law as having both a provincial and a federal aspect. See Peter W. Hogg, *Constitutional Law of Canada,* 5th ed., Supplemental, Volume 2 (Toronto: Carswell, 2007); or alternatively, the most recent Student Edition of *Constitutional Law of Canada,* Chapter 15.5.
69.   Oliver, "Busy Harbours."
70.   *Canadian Western Bank v. Alberta,* 2007 SCC 22.
71.   The determining case was *Citizens Insurance v. Parsons* in 1881.
72.   Oliver, "Busy Harbours," 178.
73.   *Alberta (Attorney General) v. Moloney,* 2015 SCC 51; *407 ETR Concession Co. v. Canada (Superintendent of Bankruptcy),* 2015 SCC 52; *Saskatchewan (Attorney General) v. Lemare Lake Logging Ltd.,* 2015 SCC 53.
74.   *Reference re Securities Act,* 2011 SCC 66.
75.   The plan included Ontario and British Columbia, but not Quebec or Alberta.

76. *Reference re Pan-Canadian Securities Regulation*, 2018 SCC 48.
77. *Quebec (Attorney General) v. Canada (Attorney General)*, 2015 SCC 14.
78. *Reference re Senate Reform*, 2014 SCC 32.
79. See Peter McCormick, Ernest Manning and Gordon Gibson, *Regional Representation* (Calgary: Canada West Foundation, 1981).
80. In 1980, the Supreme Court had set limits on the changes the Parliament alone could make to the Senate. See *Reference re Authority of Parliament in relation to the Upper House*, [1980] 1 SCR 54.
81. *Reference re Senate Reform*, 2014, SCC 32.
82. *Reference re Senate Reform*, 2014, para. 54 ff.
83. Ibid., para. 56.
84. Ibid., para. 57, quoting from *Reference re Authority of Parliament in relation to the Upper House*, 1980, p. 77.
85. *Reference re Senate Reform*, 2014, para. 57.
86. However, the decision allowed for the possible abolition of outdated property qualifications.
87. Government of Canada, *Independent Advisory Board for Senate Appointments*, https://www.canada.ca/en/campaign/independent-advisory-board-for-senate-appointments.html.
88. Bill Curry, "Senator's Poll on Senate Efficacy Draws Criticism," *The Globe and Mail*, April 12, 2019, A9. Only 3 per cent of Canadians would prefer the pre-2015 system of Senate appointments.
89. *Reference re Supreme Court Act, ss. 5 and 6*, 2014 SCC 21.
90. Ibid.
91. *Schedule to the Constitution Act*, 1982.
92. The term "constitutional architecture" is original to these two decisions on national institutions, and has raised many eyebrows. See, e.g., Emmett Macfarlane, "Unsteady Architecture: Ambiguity, the Senate Reference, and the Future of Constitutional Amendment in Canada," *McGill Law Journal* 4 (2015).
93. *Reference re Supreme Court Act*, 2014, para. 20 ff.
94. *R. v. Comeau*, 2018 SCC 15.
95. Put simply, "standards of review" refer to the question of how big an error, and what kind of error, the initial decision maker has to commit before it is appropriate for a court to alter that decision on appeal.

96.　*Dunsmuir v. New Brunswick*, 2008 SCC 9. The majority decision in this 5–4 judgment was written by Bastarache and LeBel, and McLachlin signed on to the decision.

97.　The leading decision has long been *Re Residential Tenancies Act*, [1981] 1 SCR 714.

98.　*Canadian Union of Public Employees v. New Brunswick Liquor Corporation*, [1979] 2 SCR 227.

99.　*Newfoundland and Labrador Nurses Union v. Newfoundland and Labrador (Treasury Board)*, 2011 SCC 62; *Edmonton (City) v. Edmonton East (Capilano) Shopping Centres Ltd.*, 2016 SCC 47.

100.　*Doré v. Barreau du Québec*, 2012 SCC 12; *Loyola High School v. Quebec (Attorney General)*, 2015 SCC 12.

101.　*West Fraser Mills Ltd. v. British Columbia (Workers' Compensation Appeal Tribunal)*, 2018 SCC 22. This case looks as if it was a Wagner Court decision handed down after McLachlin left the Court, but in fact this is a judgment delivered by McLachlin during the six months that a retired judge continues to deal with cases heard earlier.

102.　*Law Society of British Columbia v. Trinity Western University*, 2018 SCC 32.

103.　Robert Jacob Danay, "Quantifying Dunsmuir: An Empirical Analysis of the Supreme Court of Canada's Jurisprudence on Standard of Review," *University of Toronto Law Journal* 66 (2016): 1.

104.　See, e.g., Robert Danay, "A House Divided: The Supreme Court of Canada's Recent Jurisprudence on the Standard of Review," *University of Toronto Law Journal* 69 (2019): 3; and Matthew Lewans, "Dunsmuir's Disconnect," *University of Toronto Law Journal* 69 (2019): 18.

CHAPTER 6

1.　Editorial, "True Patriot Reason, in All of Us Command," *The Globe and Mail*, December 31, 2018, https://www.theglobeandmail.com/opinion/editorials/article-globe-editorial-true-patriot-reason-in-all-of-us-command/.

2.　Ibid.

3.　See Peter J. McCormick, "Sharing the Spotlight: Co-authored Reasons on the Modern Supreme Court of Canada," *Dalhousie Law Journal* 30 (2007): 165; and Peter J. McCormick, "Nom de Plume: Who Writes the Supreme Court's 'By the Court'

Judgments?" *Dalhousie Law Journal* 39 (2016): 77.

4.   *Carter v. Canada (Attorney General)*, 2015 SCC 5. According
        to Peter McCormick's linguistic analysis of "By the Court"
        judgements of the McLachlin court, McLachlin and Cromwell
        are the possible key authors of the *Carter* decision (McCormick,
        "Nom de Plume," 77).

5.   Dying with Dignity Canada, "Lee Carter," https://www.
        dyingwithdignity.ca/lee_carter.

6.   *Carter v. Canada*, para. 4.

7   Introduction to interview of Beverley McLachlin by Rosemary
        Barton, *CBC The National*, December 17, 2017, https://www.cbc.
        ca/player/play/1118808131669.

8.   See Greene, *Charter of Rights*, 257 ff.

9.   *Reference re ss. 193 and 195.1(1)(c) of the Criminal Code (Man.)*,
        [1990] 1 SCR 1123. McLachlin did not take part in this decision.

10.   See Edward Butts, "Robert Pickton Case," *Canadian Encyclopedia*,
        July 26, 2016, https://www.thecanadianencyclopedia.ca/en/article/
        robert-pickton-case.

11.   The three provisions of the *Criminal Code*, R.S.C. 1985, c. C-46,
        that criminalize activities related to prostitution are s. 210, which
        makes it an offence to keep or be in a bawdy-house; s. 212(1)(j),
        which prohibits living on the avails of prostitution; and s. 213(1)
        (c), which prohibits communicating in public for the purposes of
        prostitution.

12.   *Canada (Attorney General) v. Bedford*, 2013 SCC 72, para. 127.

13.   Ibid., para. 60–64. Grandma's House was shut down in 2000.

14.   *Bedford*, para. 90.

15.   *Bedford*, para. 165–69.

16.   *Canada (Attorney General) v. PHS Community Services Society*,
        2011 SCC 44, para. 4.

17.   Insite was able to stay open during the litigation period as a result
        of temporary injunctions from courts pending the final outcome
        of the litigation.

18.   *Canada v. PHS Community Services*, headnotes.

19.   *Canada (Justice) v. Khadr*, 2008 SCC 28, [2008] 2 SCR 125; and
        Canada (Prime Minister) v. Khadr, 2010 SCC 3, [2010] 1 SCR 44.
        According to McCormick's linguistic analysis, Rosalie Abella and
        Morris Fish were the possible key authors of the 2008 decision,
        and Thomas Cromwell and McLachlin were the possible co-
        authors of the 2010 decision. See McCormick, "Nom de Plume."

20.   Guantánamo Bay had been chosen by the George W. Bush
       administration to detain and "try" prisoners captured in
       Afghanistan precisely because it was not located on U.S. soil, and
       therefore, it was thought, the usual constitutional safeguards of
       due process could be ignored. In 2004 and 2006, the U.S. Supreme
       Court declared that the regime in Guantánamo Bay is illegal both
       under U.S. and international law. See *Rasul et al. v. Bush, President
       of the United States, et al.*, 542 U.S. 446 (2004), and *Hamdan v.
       Rumsfeld*, 126 S. Ct. 2749 (2006).

21.   *Khadr*, 2008, para. 2.

22.   According to the Supreme Court decision, "The [government]
       must disclose (i) all records in any form of the interviews
       conducted by Canadian officials with Mr. Khadr, and (ii)
       records of any information given to U.S. authorities as a direct
       consequence of Canada's having interviewed him. This disclosure
       is subject to the balancing of national security and other
       considerations as required by ss. 38 ff. of the Canada Evidence
       Act." *Khadr*, 2008, para. 37.

23.   Canada, Parliament, Standing Committee on Foreign Affairs
       and International Development, Subcommittee on International
       Human Rights, *Omar Khadr: Report of the Standing Committee on
       Foreign Affairs and International Development*, 39th Parliament,
       2nd Session (June 2008).

24.   Had the Harper government accepted that recommendation,
       much of the $10.5 million payout that the Canadian government
       made to Khadr in 2018 to compensate him for his mistreatment
       might have been avoided.

25.   *Khadr*, 2010, para. 25. This unanimous decision included two
       justices appointed by Stephen Harper: Marshall Rothstein and
       Thomas Cromwell.

26.   *Haida Nation v. British Columbia (Minister of Forests)*,
       2004 SCC 73.

27.   Ibid., para. 6.

28.   Ibid., para. 10.

29.   See, for example, David Ryder and Sunny Dhillon, "Unique B.C.
       Partnership Set to Restore Logged Forest of Haida Gwaii," *The
       Globe and Mail*, March 5, 2018, https://www.theglobeandmail.
       com/news/british-columbia/unique-bc-partnership-set-to-
       restore-logged-forest/article38204904/; Andrew Kurjata, "On

Haida Gwaii, Logging Plans Expose Rift in Reconciliation,
CBC News, December 9, 2017, https://www.cbc.ca/news/canada/
british-columbia/haida-gwaii-reconciliation-logging-clear-
cut-1.4429532; and Michael Mui, "B.C. Forestry Company
Responds to Over-Logging Allegations," *StarMetro Vancouver,*
June 21, 2018, https://www.thestar.com/vancouver/2018/06/21/
bc-forestry-company-responds-to-over-logging-allegations.html.

30. *Tsilhqot'in Nation v. British Columbia,* 2014 SCC 44, and *Grassy Narrows First Nation v. Ontario (Natural Resources),* 2014 SCC 48. See Greene, *Charter of Rights,* 378 ff.

31. This area is between Kamloops and Prince George, and east of Williams Lake.

32. *Tsilhqot'in Nation,* para. 7.

33. Ibid., para. 80.

34. Ibid., para. 97.

35. *Grassy Narrows First Nation v. Ontario,* para. 51–52.

36. *Ktunaxa Nation v. British Columbia (Forests, Lands and Natural Resource Operations),* 2017 SCC 54

37. *Ktunaxa,* para. 70.

38. *Ktunaxa,* para. 118–119.

39. Sean Fine, "Chief Justice Says Canada Attempted 'Cultural Genocide' on Aboriginals," *The Globe and Mail,* May 28, 2015, https://www.theglobeandmail.com/news/national/chief-justice-says-canada-attempted-cultural-genocide-on-aboriginals/article24688854/.

40. In one of her last decisions on the Supreme Court, McLachlin dissented, along with Russell Brown, from a majority decision that upheld First Nations arguments in a case dealing with compensation for historical wrongs. See *Williams Lake Indian Band v. Canada (Aboriginal Affairs and Northern Development),* 2018 SCC 4.

41. In 2017, that number was closer to 15,000. Jamil Malakieh, *Adult and Youth Correctional Statistics in Canada, 2016/2017* (Ottawa: Statistics Canada, 2018), https://www150.statcan.gc.ca/n1/pub/85-002-x/2018001/article/54972-eng.htm).

42. *Sauvé v. Canada (Attorney General),* [1993] 2 SCR 438, affirming (1992), 7 OR (3d) 481. The three-paragraph decision, which all nine judges signed on to, was written by Iacobucci.

43. *Sauvé v. Canada (Chief Electoral Officer),* [2002] 3 SCR 519, 2002 SCC 68.

44. Section 1 of the *Charter* states that "The Canadian Charter of Rights and Freedoms guarantees the rights and freedoms set out in it subject only to such reasonable limits prescribed by law as can be demonstrably justified in a free and democratic society." In the 1980s, the Supreme Court adopted the following test that governments had to pass to limit a *Charter* right: limiting the right had to be necessary to achieve an important government objective; the limit had to be rationally connected to the objective, and had to limit the right as little as necessary to achieve the objective; and the limit had to be shown to do more good than harm overall.

45. See Greene, *Charter of Rights*, 177–82.

46. Beverley McLachlin, "Fifteen Times Fifteen — Reflections on Evolution of the Court's Equality Jurisprudence," keynote address at Osgoode Hall Constitutional Cases Conference, Friday, April 6, 2001, and Rt. Hon. Beverley McLachlin, PC, "Equality: The Most Difficult Right," *Supreme Court Law Review* 14 (2001): 17, https://digitalcommons.osgoode.yorku.ca/sclr/vol14/iss1/2/.

47. *Andrews v. Law Society of British Columbia*, [1989]1 SCR 143, on appeal from [1986] 4 WWR 242.

48. *Law v. Canada (Minister of Employment and Immigration)*, [1999] 1 SCR 497.

49. *Gosselin v. Quebec (Attorney General)*, [2002] 4 SCR 429.

50. *R. v. Kapp*, [2008] 2 SCR 483.

51. *Centrale des syndicats du Québec v. Quebec (Attorney General)*, 2018 SCC 18.

CHAPTER 7

1. Ceremony on the occasion of the appointment of Beverley McLachlin as chief justice of Canada, January 7, 2000, *CBC Newsworld*.

2. We learned this in an interview with one of McLachlin's former colleagues on the Court.

3. Interview with McLachlin, April 9, 2018.

4. Ibid.

5. Interview of McLachlin by Rosemary Barton, Decmber 17, 2017.

6. Antonin Scalia, "The Dissenting Opinion" *Journal of Supreme Court History* (1994): 33. American usage employs the word opinion where Canadian usage would say judgment.

7	See Alan Paterson, *Final Judgment: The Last Law Lords and the Supreme Court* (London, U.K.: Hart Publishing, 2013).

8.	*Haaretz.com v. Goldhar*, 2018 SCC 28.

9.	*Mikisew Cree First Nation v. Canada (Governor General in Council)*, 2018 SCC 40.

10.	*Mikisew* is also a good demonstration of why separate concurrences matter. The panel was unanimous as to outcome on the basic question of the appeal (did the Federal Court have jurisdiction in the first place?), but it was divided 5–4 and 7–2 on two other issues that were important in their own right, and this will matter for later cases that focus on those other issues.

11.	This approach is more formally known as the Herfindahl-Hirschman Concentration Index. The formula is:
Index = $(a2 + b2 + c2 + \ldots) / (a + b + c + \ldots)2$
where a,b, c, . . . are the numbers of individuals in the fragments into which the panel has divided. For a unanimous and univocal decision, there is only an "a" and the two elements of the fraction are identical, for a score of 1. For the highest possible degree of division (imagine a panel of nine judges, each writing their own reasons), it becomes (1+1+1+1+1+1+1+1+1)/81, or 0.111. The double usefulness of the index for our purposes is that it represents every possible degree of panel fragmentation as a single number, while accommodating the fact that SCC practices involve varying panel sizes.

12.	See McCormick, "Second Thoughts: Supreme Court Citation of Dissents and Separate Concurrences 1949–1999," *Canadian Bar Review* 81 (2002).

13.	*Carter v. Canada (Attorney General)*, 2016 SCC 4.

14.	Before the McLachlin court era, such multiple sets of jointly authored decisions appeared only twice before in the history of the Court: the *Patriation Reference*, [1982] 2 SCR 792, and the *Alberta Natural Gas Reference*, [1982] 1 SCR 1004.

15.	There is, of course, a strong temptation to peek behind the curtain of unanimity to find the "real" lead author, if only by identifying characteristic writing styles or turns of phrase; for a more systematic attempt, see McCormick, "Nom de Plume."

16.	See Peter McCormick and Marc Zanoni, "The First 'By the Court' Decisions: The Emergence of a Practice of the Supreme Court of Canada," *Manitoba Law Journal* 38 (2015).

17.   A partial exception is the High Court of Australia, whose
       repertoire of decision delivery formats is so unusual and
       distinctive that we decline to venture into the swamp of trying
       to describe it briefly. Even there, however, we can say there is no
       practice of anonymous/unanimous judgments specifically focused
       on constitutional issues that resembles that of the SCC.

18.   The case is *Cooper v. Aaron*, 358 U.S. 1 (1958), establishing the
       status of USSC decisions regarding the interpretation of the
       United States Constitution.

19.   The case is the "Brexit decision" — *R (Miller) v. Secretary of State
       for Exiting the European Union*, 2017 UKSC 5 — which ruled
       that the U.K. government could not withdraw from the European
       Union without a formal action of the U.K. Parliament to support
       it.

20.   For a more complete account, see Peter McCormick and Marc
       D.Zanoni, *By the Court: Anonymous Judgments at the Supreme
       Court of Canada* (Vancouver: University of British Columbia
       Press, 2019).

21.   McCormick, "Nom de Plume," 77.

22.   The format is "The judgment of the Court was delivered by A and
       B" and the order of the names is always seniority.

23.   See Peter McCormick, "Sharing the Spotlight: Co-Authored
       Reasons on the Modern Supreme Court of Canada" *Dalhousie
       Law Journal* 34 (2011): 165.

24.   See Peter McCormick, "Duets, Not Solos: The McLachlin Court's
       Co-Authorship Legacy," *Dalhousie Law Journal* 41 (2018).

25.   We think this fact makes the point that co-authorship looms
       larger for the judges themselves than it might for observers like
       ourselves outside the Court.

26.   Vivian Grinfeld, "Where Are They Now? A Look at the Last 10
       Justices to Retire from the SCC," *http://www.thecourt.ca/where-
       are-they-now-a-look-at-the-last-10-justices-to-retire-from-the-scc/*
       (Osgoode Hall Law School weblog), March 21, 2019.

27.   A case in point is the very important co-authored decision
       in *Dunsmuir v. New Brunswick,* 2008 SCC 9, regarding the
       standards of review for administrative tribunals. To describe
       this case as controversial is an understatement, because it has
       provoked a decade of critical analysis with respect to its impact
       on administrative law, and there have been constant suggestions

that the Supreme Court should reconsider it. See, for example, the remarkable "digital symposium" on the Double Aspect and Administrative Law Matters weblogs, published in the *Canadian Journal of Administrative Law and Practice*, with several dozen critical mini-essays concluding with responses (solo rather than jointly authored) from each of *Dunsmuir*'s two authors (https://www.editionsyvonblais.com/detail-du-produit/canadian-journal-of-administrative-law-and-practice-and-practice-special-issue-a-decade-of-dunsmuir-les-10-ans-de-dunsmuir/).

28. "Small group theory" has been a significant component of studies of national high courts for at least sixty years. See, e.g., Eloise C. Snyder, "The Supreme Court as a Small Group" *Social Forces* 36 (1958): 232.

29. For example, there was the "L-S-D Connection" (Laskin, Spence and Dickson) in the 1970s, or the close partnership between Cory and Iacobucci in the 1990s. Cluster behaviour has been accepted as a way of understanding the Lamer Court in the form of the "gang of five" (Lamer, Sopinka, Major, Iacobucci and Cory) that generally prevailed during that period. See, e.g., Donald R. Songer, *The Transformation of the Supreme Court of Canada: An Empirical Examination* (Toronto; University of Toronto Press, 2008), 192; and Backhouse, *Claire L'Heureux-Dubé*, 651.

30. Large differences in these proportions may begin to identify the leaders of the Court, and a "spread" within the table could be a first hint as to the membership of an "in group" and "out group."

31. See Peter McCormick, "Birds of a Feather: Alliances and Influences on the Lamer court 1991–7," *Osgoode Hall Law Journal* 36 (1998); and Peter McCormick "Follow the Leader: Judicial Leadership and the Laskin Court 1973–1984," *Queen's Law Journal* 24 (1998).

32. Interview with McLachlin, April 9, 2018.

33. Joseph Brean, "'Conscious Objectivity': That's How the Chief Justice Defines the Top Court's Role. Harper Might Beg to Differ," *National Post*, May 23, 2015, https://nationalpost.com/news/conscious-objectivity-thats-how-the-chief-justice-defines-the-top-courts-role-harper-might-beg-to-differ.

34. See Peter McCormick, "Voting Blocs on the McLachlin Court, 2000–2010," paper presented at the Canadian Political Science Association annual meeting (Congress of the Humanities and Social Sciences), Montreal, June 2010.

35.   It is not impossible for a chief justice to be outside the Court's dominant group, frequently obliged to dissent vigorously; that was true of Bora Laskin for the first half of his chief justiceship.

36.   Interview with McLachlin, April 9, 2018.

37.   See Peter McCormick "'Was it Something I Said?' Losing the Majority on the Supreme Court of Canada," *Osgoode Hall Law Journal* 59 (2012).

38.   The name of the writer was less often mentioned if you cited a case without quotation.

39.   From another perspective, citations help to write a heroic history, with the respectfully cited names of outstanding judges identifying the heroes who are featured in the story.

40.   Interview with McLachlin, April 9, 2018.

41.   On several occasions, this development has reached its logical end point: judgments of normal length, with the usual dozen or so citations of previous Supreme Court decisions often including direct quotation, but not a single one of them including the name of the judge being cited or quoted. As recently as twenty years ago, such a possibility was beyond contemplation.

42.   This does not count the two decisions that were "By the Court," which would have pushed the count even higher.

43.   Interview with McLachlin, April 9, 2018.

44.   Carol Gilligan, *In a Different Voice: Psychological Theory and Women's Development* (Cambridge, MA: Harvard University Press, 1982).

45.   Interview with McLachlin, April 9, 2018.

46.   Scalia famously described majority opinions he disagreed with as "pure applesauce" and "jiggery pokery" (*King v. Burwell*) and as "the mystical aphorisms of the fortune cookie" (*Obergefell v. Hodges*). He easily topped the "sarcasm index" of USSC justices; see Richard L. Hasen, "The Most Sarcastic Justice," *Green Bag* 18, no. 2 (2015): 215.

47.   Like Scalia's charge in *Atkins v. Virginia*, "Seldom has an opinion of this Court rested so obviously upon nothing but the personal views of its members."

48.   Justice Louis LeBel, lunch-time speech, April 11, 2018, at University of Ottawa Faculty of Law, Common Law Section, and Canadian Institute for the Administration of Justice conference, "Reflecting on the Legacy of Chief Justice McLachlin," April 10-11, 2018.

49. Pamela C. Corley, Amy Steigerwalt and Artemus Ward, *The Puzzle of Unanimity: Consensus on the United States Supreme Court* (Stanford, CA: Stanford Law Books, 2013).

CHAPTER 8

1. See W.R. Lederman, "The Independence of the Judiciary," *Canadian Bar Review* 34 (1956): 769.

2. Judicial independence is incorporated into the Canadian Constitution through the preamble to the *Constitution Act, 1867,* the preamble to the Canadian *Charter of Rights and Freedoms* (Schedule B to Canada Act 1982), and with regard to those "charged with an offence," by section 11(d) of the *Charter of Rights and Freedoms.*

3. The incidents involved Jean Chrétien in 1971, and Bud Drury in 1976. Also in 1976, it was revealed that cabinet minister Marc Lalonde, when serving as principal secretary to the prime minister in 1970, made inappropriate contact with a judge. See McCormick and Greene, *Judges and Judging* (Toronto: Lorimer, 1991), 248–49, and Peter Russell, *The Judiciary in Canada* (Toronto: McGraw-Hill Ryerson, 1987), 78–79.

4. Robert Lewis, "The Short Penance of Bud Drury," *Maclean's,* March 22, 1976, https://archive.macleans.ca/article/1976/3/22/the-short-penance-of-bud-drury.

5. These were John Munro in 1978, and Jean Charest in 1989. See Brian Bergman, "Breach of the code: The 10th Tory Cabinet Minister Steps Down," *Maclean's,* February 5, 1990, https://archive.macleans.ca/article/1990/2/5/breach-of-the-code, and Michael Posner, "Act in Haste, Repent at Leisure," *Maclean's,* September 18, 1978, https://archive.macleans.ca/article/1978/9/18/act-in-haste-repent-at-leisure.

6. See Audrey Macklin and Lorne Waldman, "When Cabinet Ministers Attack Judges, They Attack Democracy," *The Globe and Mail,* February 18, 2011, https://www.theglobeandmail.com/opinion/when-cabinet-ministers-attack-judges-they-attack-democracy/article566845/.

7 *Quebec Act, 1774 (U.K.),* RSC 1985, Appendix II, No. 2. See Peter H. Russell, *Canada's Odyssey: A Country Based on Incomplete Conquests* (Toronto: University of Toronto Press, 2017), 30–31.

8. *Constitution Act, 1867,* s. 92(13), "Property and Civil Rights."

9.   John Ivison, "Tories Incensed with Supreme Court as Some
        Allege Chief Justice Lobbied Against Marc Nadon Appointment,"
        National Post, May 1, 2014, https://nationalpost.com/news/
        politics/tories-incensed-with-supreme-court-as-some-allege-
        chief-justice-lobbied-against-marc-nadon-appointment.

10.   According to a 2014 survey, the *Charter of Rights* was the first
        choice of a plurality of Canadians who were asked to choose
        among eleven items that keep Canada united. See Benjamin
        Shingler, "Charter of Rights and Universal Health Care Unites
        Canadians: Poll," Canadian Press, http://www.ctvnews.ca/canada/
        charter-of-rights-and-universal-health-care-unites-canadians-
        poll-1.1892818.

11.   For example, Rainer Knopff and F. L. Morton, *Charter Politics*
        (Toronto: Nelson, 1992), and Michael Mandel, *The Charter
        of Rights and the Legalization of Politics in Canada* (Toronto:
        Thompson Educational Publishing, 1992). For an overview and
        critique of this early *Charter* literature, see Peter H. Russell,
        "The Charter and Canadian Democracy," in James B. Kelly and
        Christopher P. Manfredi, eds., *Contested Constitutionalism:
        Reflections on the Canadian Charter of Rights and Freedoms*
        (Vancouver: University of British Columbia Press, 2009), 287.

12.   These interviews are analyzed in Greene et al., *Final Appeal*, and
        McCormick and Greene, *Judges and Judging.*The attitude of these
        judges is well captured by the title of one of Supreme Court Justice
        Bertha Wilson's articles,"We Didn't Volunteer," *Policy Options*
        (April, 1999), p. 8.

13.   Jeffrey B. Meyers, "First Ontario, Now Quebec: The
        Notwithstanding Threat," *Conversation*, October 10, 2018,
        https://theconversation.com/first-ontario-now-quebec-the-
        notwithstanding-threat-104379.

14.   Ivison, "Tories Incensed with Supreme Court."

15.   *Canada (Justice) v. Khadr*, 2008 SCC 28, [2008] 2 SCR 125; and
        Canada (Prime Minister) v. Khadr, 2010 SCC 3, [2010] 1 SCR 44.

16.   *Reference re Securities Act*, 2011 SCC 66.

17.   *Canada (Attorney General) v. PHS Community Services Society*,
        2011 SCC 44.

18.   *R. v. Clarke*, 2014 SCC 28; *R. v. Summes*, [2014] 1 SCR 575; and *R.
        v. Carvery*, [2014] 1 SCR 605.

19.   Sean Fine, "The Secret Short List that Provoked the Rift Between

Chief Justice and PMO," *The Globe and Mail*, May 23, 2014 (updated February23, 2016), http://www.theglobeandmail.com/ news/politics/the-secret-short-list-that-caused-a-rift-between- chief-justice-and-pmo/article18823392/?page=all.

20.   Fine, "Secret Short List," and John Ibbitson, *Stephen Harper* (Toronto: Signal, McClelland & Stewart, 2015), location 6684 ff.

21.   Ibid. The Court of Appeal judges were Justice Marie-France Bich and Justice Pierre Dalphond.

22.   Supreme Court of Canada, News Release, May 2, 2014, https:// scc-csc.lexum.com/scc-csc/news/en/item/4602/index.do.

23.   Interview with Peter Russell by Ian Greene, February 20, 2016.

24.   "Timeline: Marc Nadon's Failed Journey to the Supreme Court: The Failed Process of Naming Nadon to the Highest Court in the Land Started Over a Year Ago," Canadian Press, May 8 2014, http://www.cbc.ca/news/politics/marc-nadon-s-failed-journey-to- the-supreme-court-1.2636403.

25.   Lawyer Paul Slansky later joined the litigation in support of Galati's argument.

26.   For example, Galati was Abdurahman Khadr's first lawyer in Canada. Abdurahman Khadr was Omar Khadr's older brother who claimed that he became a CIA agent.

27.   Marc Nadon was appointed to the trial division of the Federal Court in 1993, and the appeal division in 2001.

28.   *Supreme Court Act*, RSC 1985, c. S-26.

29.   Sections 5.1 and 6.1 were added to Sections 5 and 6 of the *Supreme Court Act*.

30.   *Reference re Supreme Court Act*, ss. 5 and 6, 2014 SCC 21.

31.   See "Royal Commission on Bilingualism and Biculturalism," *Canadian Encyclopedia*, https://www.thecanadianencyclopedia.ca/ en/article/royal-commission-on-bilingualism-and-biculturalism.

32.   Peter H. Russell, *The Supreme Court of Canada as a Bilingual and Bicultural Institution* (1969), at p. 8.

33.   Ivison, "Tories Incensed with Supreme Court."

34.   According to Tom Flanagan, who had been one of Harper's senior advisors up to 2004, "He believes in playing politics right up to the edge of the rules, which inevitably means some team members will step across ethical or legal lines in their desire to win for the Boss. He can be . . . prone to sudden eruptions of white-hot rage over meaningless trivia." Tom Flanagan, *Persona Non Grata: The*

Death of Free Speech in the Internet Age (Toronto: McClelland & Stewart, Kindle Edition, 2014), 29.

35.   Sean Fine, "Chief Justice Hits Back at Prime Minister Over Claim of Improper Call," *The Globe and Mail*, May 2, 2014, https://www.theglobeandmail.com/news/politics/chief-justice-denies-allegations-of-improper-contact-with-pmo/article18397514/.

36.   Ibid.

37.   Fine, "How Beverley McLachlin Found Her Bliss," at A15.

38.   Ibid.

39.   Supreme Court of Canada, News Release, May 2, 2014.

40.   Robert Sharpe and Kent Roach, *Brian Dickson: A Judge's Journey* (Toronto: Osgoode Society / University of Toronto Press, 2013), 298.

41.   Ibid.

42.   Ibbitson, op. cit., location 6718.

43.   Laura Payton, "Brian Mulroney Says Supreme Court Criticism 'Sends Wrong Signal,'" *CBC News*, September 5, 2014, https://www.cbc.ca/news/politics/brian-mulroney-says-supreme-court-criticism-sends-wrong-signal-1.2756734, and Tonda MacCharles, "Joe Clark, Paul Martin Criticize PM's Attack on Chief Justice," *Toronto Star*, May 20, 2014, https://www.thestar.com/news/canada/2014/05/20/joe_clark_paul_martin_criticize_pms_attack_on_chief_justice.html.

44.   Mark Kennedy, "International Panel Slams Stephen Harper for Treatment of Supreme Court Justice," *Ottawa Citizen*, July 25, 2014, http://ottawacitizen.com/news/national/international-jurists-slam-stephen-harper-for-his-treatment-of-supreme-court-justice.

45.   According to law professor Jamie Cameron, this "rash and astonishing attack on the Chief Justice . . . was the most extraordinary event of 2014 [for the Supreme Court], if not the Court's entire institutional history." Jamie Cameron, "Law, Politics and Legacy Building at the McLachlin Court in 2014," *Supreme Court Law Review: Osgoode's Annual Constitutional Cases Conference* 71 (2015), 7, http://digitalcommons.osgoode.yorku.ca/sclr/vol71/iss1/1. In a book that is generally positive about Harper, *The Globe and Mail* journalist John Ibbitson calls Harper's broadside one of his "most discreditable acts as prime minister." John Ibbitson, *Stephen Harper*

(Toronto: Signal, McClelland & Stewart, 2015), location 6727.

46. Grant Duncan, "New Zealand's Cabinet Manual: How Does It Shape Constitutional Conventions?" *Parliamentary Affairs* 68 (2015): 737–56, and "The Cabinet Office Manual," *Te Ara: The Enclycopedia of New Zealand*, https://teara.govt.nz/en/zoomify/34352/the-cabinet-office-manual. The United Kingdom has recently produced a similar document for the guidance of politicians.

47. New Zealand, Department of the Prime Minister and Cabinet, *Cabinet Manual 2017, Sections 4.12 and 4.13, 58*, https://dpmc.govt.nz/our-business-units/cabinet-office/supporting-work-cabinet/cabinet-manual.

CHAPTER 9

1. It should be noted that during the McLachlin era, occasionally the chief justice would call for a second conference (or meeting of the judges) about a particular case. These second conferences were rare, if not non-existent, prior to McLachlin.

2. Singapore, PMO Press Release, "Appointments/Reappointments to the Singapore International Commercial Court," https://www.supremecourt.gov.sg/news/media-releases/pmo-press-release--appointmentsreappointments-to-the-singapore-international-commercial-court.

3. Peter Zimonjic, "Former Supreme Court of Canada Chief Justice Beverley McLachlin to be Judge in Hong Kong," *CBC News*, March 21, 2018, https://www.cbc.ca/news/politics/beverley-mclachlin-hong-kong-1.4587221.

4. Interview with McLachlin, April 9, 2018.

5. In the American literature, the standard example is the USSC's Justice William O. Douglas, who served on the Court from 1939 to 1975.

6. Which explains the title of Noah Feldman's book *Scorpions: The Battles and Triumphs of FDR's Great Supreme Court Justices* (New York; Hachette Book Group, 2010).

7 Supreme Court of Canada, "Statistical Summary 2008-2018," retrieved from https://www.scc-csc.ca/case-dossier/stat/sum-som-2018-eng.aspx. In 2018, the proportion of unanimous judgments dropped to just 48 per cent, the lowest in ten years.

8. Justice Henry Grattan Nolan died soon after his appointment.

9.   In 1974, Parliament reformed the pension regime for federally appointed judges, which made early retirement more attractive. See *Beauregard v. Canada*, [1986] 2 SCR 56.

10.   Interview with McLachlin, April 9, 2018.

11.   Ibid.

12.   Ibid.

13.   Ibid.

14.   Ibid.

15.   Jeffrey B. Meyers, "First Ontario, Now Quebec: The Notwithstanding Threat," *Conversation*, October 10, 2018, https://theconversation.com/first-ontario-now-quebec-the-notwithstanding-threat-104379.

16.   Ibid.

Bibliography

Ashenburg, Katherine, "Canada's Top Judge: Chief Justice Beverley McLachlin's Remarkable Service," *Alberta Views*, September 2016, 35, at 36.

Backhouse, Constance, *Claire L'Heureux-Dubé: A Life* (Vancouver: University of British Columbia Press / Osgoode Society, 2017).

Beaton, Ryan, *The Crown Fiduciary Duty at the Supreme Court of Canada*, Canada in International Law at 150 and Beyond, Paper No.6 (Waterloo, ON: Centre for International Governance Innovation, January 2018).

Belanger Yale D. and P. Whitney Lackenbaur, eds., *Blockades or Breakthroughs?: Aboriginal Peoples Confront the Canadian State* (Montreal: McGill-Queen's University Press, 2014).

Belleau, Marie-Clare, Rebecca Johnson and Valerie Bouchard, "Faces of Judicial Anger: Answering the Call," in Myriam Jézéquel and Nicolas Kasirer, eds., *Les sept péchés capitaux et le droit privé* (Montreal; Les editions Thémis, 2007).

Brean, Joseph, "'Conscious Objectivity': That's How the Chief Justice Defines the Top Court's Role. Harper Might Beg to Differ," *National Post*, May 23, 2015.

Cameron, Jamie, "McLachlin's Law: In All Its Complex Majesty," *Supreme Court Law Review* 88 (2019) (2d), 307–41.

Cameron, Jamie, "A Review of the Supreme Court's 2018 Constitutional Jurisprudence," *Osgoode Hall Annual Constitutional Cases Conference*, April 5, 2019.

Cameron, Jamie, "Law, Politics and Legacy Building at the McLachlin Court in 2014," *Supreme Court Law Review: Osgoode's Annual Constitutional Cases Conference*, 71 (2015).

Cheffins, R.I., "The Supreme Court of Canada: The Quiet Court in an Unquiet Country," *Osgoode Hall Law Journal* 4 (1966).

Corley, Pamela C., Amy Steigerwalt and Artemus Ward, *The Puzzle of Unanimity: Consensus on the United States Supreme Court* (Stanford, CA: Stanford Law Books, 2013).

Curry, Bill, "Chief Justice Beverley McLachlin Takes Pride in Work on Indigenous rights as She Retires," *The Globe and Mail*, December 15, 2017.

Danay, Robert, "A House Divided: The Supreme Court of Canada's Recent Jurisprudence on the Standard of Review," *University of Toronto Law Journal* 69 (2019), 3.

Danay, Robert, "Quantifying *Dunsmuir*: An Empirical Analysis of the Supreme Court of Canada's Jurisprudence on Standard of Review," *University of Toronto Law Journal* 66 (2016): 1.

Feldman, Noah, *Scorpions: The Battles and Triumphs of FDR's Great Supreme Court Justices* (New York; Hachette Book Group, 2010)

Feniak, Peter, "Profile Beverley McLachlin: From the Supreme Court to the Bestseller List," *Good Times*, September 2018, 10.

Fine, Sean, "Chief Justice Hits Back at Prime Minister Over Claim of Improper Call," *The Globe and Mail*, May 2, 2014.

Fine, Sean, "How Beverley McLachlin Found Her Bliss," *The Globe and Mail*, January 13, 2018, A12.

Fine, Sean, "The Secret Short List that Provoked the Rift Between Chief Justice and PMO," *The Globe and Mail*, May 23, 2014 (updated February 23, 2016).

Fuller, Lon L., "Positivism and Fidelity to Law — A Reply to Professor Hart," *Harvard Law Review* 71 (1958): 630.

Greene, Ian, *The Charter of Rights and Freedoms: 30+ Years of Decisions That Shape Canadian Life* (Toronto: Lorimer, 2014).

Greene, Ian, *The Courts* (Vancouver: University of British Columbia Press, 2006).

Greene, Ian and David P. Shugarman, *Honest Politics Now: What Ethical Conduct Means in Canadian Public Life* (Toronto: Lorimer, 2017).

Greene, Ian, Carl Baar, Peter McCormick, George Szablowski and Martin Thomas, *Final Appeal: Decision-making in Canadian Courts of Appeal* (Toronto: Lorimer, 1998).

Grinfeld, Vivian, "Where Are They Now? A Look at the Last 10 Justices to Retire from the SCC," *TheCourt.ca* (Osgoode Hall Law School weblog), March 21, 2019.

Hart, H.L.A., *The Concept of Law* (Oxford, U.K.: Oxford University Press, 1961).

Hasen, Richard L., "The Most Sarcastic Justice," *Green Bag* 18, no. 2 (2015): 215.

Heard, Andrew, "The *Charter* in the Supreme Court of Canada: The Importance of Which Judges Hear an Appeal," *Canadian Journal of Political Science* 24 (1991): 289.

Hogg, Peter W., *Constitutional Law of Canada*, 5th ed. Supplemental, Volume 2, (Toronto: Carswell, 2007).

Ibbitson, John, *Stephen Harper* (Toronto: Signal, McClelland & Stewart, 2015).

Izard, Ian D. "The *Charter* and Electoral Law in British Columbia," *Canadian Parliamentary Review* 23 (Winter 1989–1990).

Kennedy, Mark, "International Panel Slams Stephen Harper for Treatment of Supreme Court Justice," *Ottawa Citizen*, July 25, 2014.

Knopff, Rainer and F. L. Morton, *Charter Politics* (Toronto: Nelson, 1992).

Lewans, Matthew, "*Dunsmuir's* Disconnect," *University of Toronto Law Journal* 69 (2019), 18.

MacCharles, Tonda, "Joe Clark, Paul Martin Criticize PM's Attack on Chief Justice," *Toronto Star*, May 20, 2014.

Macfarlane, Emmett, "Unsteady Architecture: Ambiguity, the Senate Reference, and the Future of Constitutional Amendment in Canada," *McGill Law Journal* 4 (2015).

McLachlin, Beverley, "And Then Fate Intervened," *The Globe and Mail*, April 28, 2018, 18.

McLachlin, Beverley, "Equality: The Most Difficult Right," *Supreme Court Law Review* 14 (2001): 17.

McLachlin, Beverley, "Fifteen Times Fifteen — Reflections on Evolution of the Court's Equality Jurisprudence," keynote address at Osgoode Hall Constitutional Cases Conference, Friday, April 6, 2001.

McLachlin, Beverley, *Full Disclosure* (Toronto: Simon & Schuster, 2018).

McLachlin, Beverley, "How I Became a Thriller Writer," *The Globe and Mail*, April 26, 2018.

McLachlin, Beverley M., and James P. Taylor, *British Columbia Practice* (Vancouver: Butterworths, 1979).

McLachlin, Beverley M., and Wilfred J. Wallace, *The Canadian Law of Architecture and Engineering* (Toronto and Vancouver: Butterworths, 1987).

McCormick, Peter, "Birds of a Feather: Alliances and Influences on the Lamer Court 1991-7" *Osgoode Hall Law Journal* 36 (1998), 339.

McCormick, Peter, *Canada's Courts* (Toronto: Lorimer, 1994).

McCormick, Peter, "Choosing the Chief: Alternation, Duality and Beyond," *Osgoode Hall Law Journal* 47 (2013): 5.

McCormick, Peter, "Duets, Not Solos: The McLachlin Court's Co-Authorship Legacy," *Dalhousie Law Journal* 41 (2018).

McCormick, Peter, *The End of the Charter Revolution* (Toronto: University of Toronto Press, 2015).

McCormick, Peter, "Follow the Leader: Judicial Leadership and the Laskin Court 1973–1984," *Queen's Law Journal* 24 (1998).

McCormick, Peter, "How Should Justin Trudeau Choose the Next Chief Justice of the Supreme Court?" *Policy Options*, November 25, 2015.

McCormick, Peter, "New Questions about an Old Concept: The Supreme Court of Canada's Judicial Independence," *Canadian Journal of Political Science* 37, no. 4 (December 2004): 839–62.

McCormick, Peter, "*Nom de Plume:* Who Writes the Supreme Court's 'By the Court' Judgments?" *Dalhousie Law Journal* 29 (2016).

McCormick, Peter, "Second Thoughts: Supreme Court Citation of Dissents and Separate Concurrences 1949–1999," *Canadian Bar Review* 81 (2002).

McCormick, Peter, "Selecting the Supremes: The Appointment of Judges to the Supreme Court of Canada," *Journal of Appellate Practice and Process* 7 (2005): 1.

McCormick, Peter, "Sharing the Spotlight: Co-Authored Reasons on the Modern Supreme Court of Canada," *Dalhousie Law Journal* 34 (2011): 165.

McCormick, Peter, *Supreme at Last: The Evolution of the Supreme Court of Canada* (Toronto: Lorimer, 2000).

McCormick, Peter, "Voting Blocs on the McLachlin Court, 2000–2010," paper presented at the Canadian Political Science Association annual meeting (Congress of the Humanities and Social Sciences), Montreal, June 2010.

McCormick, Peter, "Who Writes? Gender and Judgment Assignment on the Supreme Court of Canada," *Osgoode Hall Law Journal* 51 (2014), 595.

McCormick, Peter and Ian Greene, *Judges and Judging: Inside the Canadian Judicial System* (Toronto: Lorimer, 1990).

McCormick, Peter, Ernest Manning and Gordon Gibson, *Regional Representation* (Calgary: Canada West Foundation, 1981).

McCormick, Peter, and Marc D. Zanoni, *By the Court: Anonymous Judgments at the Supreme Court of Canada* (Vancouver: University of British Columbia Press, 2019).

McCormick, Peter and Marc Zanoni, "The First 'By the Court' Decisions: The Emergence of a Practice of the Supreme Court of Canada," *Manitoba Law Journal* 38 (2015).

Macklin, Audrey, and Waldman, Lorne, "When Cabinet Ministers Attack Judges, They Attack Democracy," *The Globe and Mail*, February 18, 2011.

Macleod, Rod, *All True Things: A History of the University of Alberta* (Edmonton: University of Alberta Press, 2008), 155 ff.

Makin, Kirk, "Beverley McLachlin," *Canadian Encyclopedia*, January 29, 2008.

Mandel, Michael, *The Charter of Rights and the Legalization of Politics in Canada* (Toronto: Thompson Educational Publishing, 1992).

Matthews, Sheelagh, "From Pincher Creek to the Supreme Court: Chief Justice Beverley McLachlin's Story," *Lethbridge Living*, Summer 2000, 20.

Meyers, Jeffrey B., "First Ontario, Now Quebec: The Notwithstanding Threat," *The Conversation*, October 10, 2018.

Mui, Michael, "B.C. Forestry Company Responds to Over-Logging Allegations," *StarMetro Vancouver*, June 21, 2018.

Oliver, Peter C., "The Busy Harbours of Canadian Federalism: The Division of Powers and Its Doctrines in the McLachlin Court," in David A. Wright and Adam Dodek, eds., *Public Law at the McLachlin Court: The First Decade* (Toronto: Irwin Law, 2011).

Paterson, Alan, *Final Judgment: The Last Law Lords and the Supreme Court* (London, U.K.: Hart Publishing; 2013).

Payton, Laura, "Brian Mulroney Says Supreme Court Criticism 'Sends Wrong Signal,'" *CBC News*, September 5, 2014.

Pue, W. Wesley, *A History of British Columbia Legal Education*, University of British Columbia Legal History Papers, WP 2000-1 (March 2000), 212.

Russell, Peter H., *Canada's Odyssey: A Country Based on Incomplete Conquests* (Toronto: University of Toronto Press, 2017).

Russell, Peter H., "The *Charter* and Canadian Democracy," in James B. Kelly and Christopher P. Manfredi, eds., *Contested Constitutionalism: Reflections on the Canadian Charter of Rights and Freedoms* (Vancouver: University of British Columbia Press, 2009), 287.

Russell, Peter H., *The Judiciary in Canada* (Toronto: McGraw-Hill Ryerson, 1987).

Ryder, David and Sunny Dhillon, "Unique B.C. Partnership Set to Restore Logged Forest of Haida Gwaii," *The Globe and Mail*, March 5, 2018.

Sanderson, Chris, W., Keith B. Bergner and Michelle S. Jones, "The Crown's Duty to Consult Aboriginal Peoples: Towards an

Understanding of the Source, Purpose and Limits of the Duty," *Alberta Law Review* 49 (2012).

Scalia, Antonin, "The Dissenting Opinion," *Journal of Supreme Court History* (1994): 33.

Shaffer, Martha, "*Seaboyer v. R.*: A Case Comment," *Canadian Journal of Women and the Law* 5 (1992): 202.

Sharpe, Robert and Kent Roach, *Brian Dickson: A Judge's Journey* (Toronto: Osgoode Society /University of Toronto Press, 2013), 298.

Slayton, Philip, *Mighty Judgment: How the Supreme Court of Canada Runs Your Life* (Toronto: Allen Lane Canada, 2011).

Slotnick, Elliot E., "Who Speaks for the Court? Majority Opinion Assignment from Taft to Burger," *American Journal of Political Science* 23 (1979), 60.

Songer, Donald R., *The Transformation of the Supreme Court of Canada: An Empirical Examination* (Toronto; University of Toronto Press, 2008), 192.

Williams, David Ricardo, *Duff: A Life in the Law* (Vancouver: University of British Columbia Press, 1984), 74.

Wilson, Bertha, "We Didn't Volunteer," *Policy Options* (April, 1999): 8.

Index